Comic Books and America, 1945-1954

Comic Books and America, 1945-1954

by William W. Savage, Jr.

University of Oklahoma Press : Norman and London

By William W. Savage, Jr.

The Cherokee Strip Live Stock Association: Federal Regulation and the Cattleman's Last Frontier (Columbia, Mo., 1973; Norman, 1990)

(ed.) *Cowboy Life: Reconstructing an American Myth* (Norman, 1975)

(ed., with David Harry Miller) *The Character and Influence of the Indian Trade in Wisconsin: A Study of the Trading Post as an Institution*, by Frederick Jackson Turner (Norman, 1977)

(ed.) *Indian Life: Transforming an American Myth* (Norman, 1977)

(ed., with Stephen I. Thompson) *The Frontier: Comparative Studies*, Vol. 2 (Norman, 1979)

The Cowboy Hero: His Image in American History and Culture (Norman, 1979)

Singing Cowboys and All That Jazz: A Short History of Popular Music in Oklahoma (Norman, 1983)

El Heroe Cowboy, trans. by Graciela Arancibia (Buenos Aires, 1985)

Comic Books and America, 1945–1954 (Norman, 1990)

Library of Congress Cataloging-in-Publication Data

Savage, William W.
    Comic books and America, 1945–1954 / by William W. Savage, Jr.—1st ed.
        p.   cm.
    Includes bibliographical references and index.
    ISBN 0-8061-2305-2 (alk. paper)
    1. United States—Popular culture—History—20th century.   2. Comic books, strips, etc.—United States—History—20th century.   I. Title.
E169.12.S293   1990
306.4'88—dc20   90-50238
                                                              CIP

For Sheila

Contents

Preface

Comic *Books and America* proceeds from a series of assumptions concerning the primacy of the comic book as an artifact of popular culture in the first decade after World War II. The assertion is that comic books in the postwar decade, through a unique combination of text and pictures, offered a world-view to a large segment of the American population (primarily children and adolescents, but, as we shall see, some adults as well) that did not as yet have one. The world after 1945, as historians are wont to say, was a more confusing place that it had ever been before; and Americans generally were at some pains to explain their position in it. Comic books, like other products of mass culture, comprised one vehicle for explanation.

Comic books did their most memorable work at a time when American society was experiencing intense and prolonged stress stemming from problems of postwar adjustment. Americans had not only to confront the potentialities of life in the atomic age, the perceived threat of world domination by Communists of several nationalities, and, by 1950, a new war in a strange place named Korea; they had also to deal with the meaning of a spiraling divorce rate, forecasts of the demise of the family as a basic American institution, and public preoccupation with issues ranging from juvenile delinquency to homosexuality to organized crime. That Dad's newspaper and Mom's magazine spoke regularly to these matters is widely acknowledged by students of the postwar period; but that Junior's comic book addressed them too is rarely recognized. Indeed, it was precisely the concern of comic books with controversial issues that brought them under scrutiny by critics who decried their pernicious influence on young minds. By 1954, the sound and fury of the critical attack drove most comic-book publishers out of business and resulted, until about 1980, in a sanitized, if not sterile, product that avoided social commentary as if it were the plague.

Comic Books and America seeks to enhance our understanding of the cultural context of a postwar generation of young readers that has long since come of age, experienced its own war, borne and reared its own children, and, now in its middle years, has assumed its place as the generation with power to effect change. *Comic Books and America* should demonstrate anew that even the most ephemeral and seemingly inconsequential literature—and in most quarters the comic book was certainly that—can tell us a great deal about the society that produced and harbored it. Children may have read the books, but adults wrote and drew them; and from that symbiosis a synthesis of the period may emerge—not to stand alone, to be sure, but to be employed in existing contexts to contribute to our understanding of who we were, and, it follows, who we are. In this instance, the child is indeed father of the man.

Scholars who tend toward cultural elitism will blanch at the notion, but *Comic Books and America* is rather like intellectual history—except that intellectual history often concerns things that seldom if ever influenced very many people at once. The least of the comic books cited here probably, in its day, touched more people than any of the classic texts promoting any of the "isms" by which the academy measures the convolutions of the American mind. I am simply suggesting another category of documentation, another window on the American experience; and I would urge skeptics to recall the time, not long ago, when the relationship between history and, say, the cinema would have been considered inappropriate for scholarly discourse. In short, if the material exists and can be useful, why not use it?

Comic Books and America is not a history of comic books. It is an initial effort to employ comic books as primary sources in the contexts outlined above, and in connection with topics of concern in postwar America. In that regard, I have chosen to discuss artists, writers, editors, and publishers generically. Where individuals are discussed, it is because they have had something to say about the subjects at hand, or because they are identified with particular themes. The notes contain information concerning the whereabouts of some testimony from the creators of comic books. Fortunately, more and more material of this sort is becoming available; but because my interests here are with content rather than style or any other aesthetic consideration, I confess to having exploited it sparingly. Many comic books of the era were produced as work-for-hire by comic "shops," actually studios employing both artists and writers who might labor there for a year or two before moving on. Under the circumstances, and given the widespread use of *noms de plume,* identification of artists is difficult enough. The accurate assignment of responsibility for editorial content is virtually impossible. Extensive lists of "credits" on the splash pages of comic books are relatively recent phenomena—they have tended to grow in the past few years in the same way that motion picture and television credits have. But in the 1940s and 1950s, few such conveniences were provided.

The question of sources and their availability will be treated at greater length in the Bibliographical Essay below, but at the moment I am compelled to prepare the reader for the contemplation of my documentation. There were, in the postwar decade, between 500 and 650 comic-book titles appearing monthly, representing a total production, some have claimed, of 60 million copies per month. I might easily have produced a section of notes sufficient to occupy several separate volumes, but in view of the indispensable indexes compiled by Robert M. Overstreet, that would be superfluous. The point to remember is that each item cited in *Comic Books and*

America represents dozens, if not literally hundreds, of others. While I have perused thousands of comic books in the preparation of this study, I have not read *all* comic books; nor do I think that such an adventure is necessary. Indeed, I have not pursued every theme represented by comic books of the period. I have discussed those which illuminate topics of concern during the decade—topics treated in other media and therefore reflective of national concerns. And I have given them the relative weight they seemed to possess at the time. In other words, I have not imposed the concerns of the present upon a past that had not yet arrived at any great awareness of them. I do not say that there is no place for such an approach, but I am saying that I think it would be inappropriate here. Women and minorities, to list but two examples, are discussed within topics relevant to the postwar decade and do not receive separate chapters because to treat them in that manner would be to distort the concerns of those times. My hope is that material contained herein will lend itself to future works dealing with, say, women and minorities. The cart travels best that follows the horse.

My debts, while few, are profound. I must acknowledge the invaluable assistance of Bart Bush, an authority on the history of comic books, a noted collector, and a dealer of unsurpassed integrity. But for his persistence in tracking the elusive copy of this-or-that, I might never have had an opportunity to examine any number of key items. I am grateful also to Linda Reese, a diligent researcher who generously shared with me the results of her investigations into the social fabric of the 1950s. And I cannot forget my friend James H. Lazalier, a rare historian who does not automatically chuckle when the subject is popular culture, who shared in this instance his insights into Korea and the Cold War and saved me from errors more than once. Barbara Million, Martha Penisten, and Amy Forwoodson suffered through my handwriting yet again and typed the manuscript with customary aplomb. Jack E. Wardlow, III, and Marsha L. Weisiger assisted with proofreading chores. To all these, I offer my thanks. I express my gratitude as well to Marvel Entertainment Group, Inc., for its kind permission to reprint two stories from *Kent Blake of the Secret Service* and *Battlefield.*

My greatest debt is to my wife, to whom this book is dedicated. Without her, neither it nor a good many other things would have been possible.

WILLIAM W. SAVAGE, JR.

Norman, Oklahoma

Comic Books
and America,
1945-1954

1

Introduction: The Rise and Decline of Escapism, 1929-1945

During the 1930s, purveyors of popular culture offered escape to the American people. Perhaps they were simply trying to ease Americans through a difficult time by making no offensive reference to the extent of economic calamity wrought by the Depression. If so, the tactic led them conveniently away from the arena of social commentary and thus from the taint of controversy. Concern over Communist activity (the legacy of the Red Scare of the 1920s), distrust of some labor unions, and reaction to even the vaguest of utterances suggestive of socialist sentiment in response to the perceived collapse of capitalism—easy enough to imagine in the 1930s—had all worked toward the kind of consensus that made most social (and necessarily, political and economic) criticism suspect. So, whether the Depression was too dangerous to contemplate or merely too unpleasant, popular culture tended to focus on either the past or the future. Rarely did it examine the present in any relevant manner.[1]

In films—and they are the sole consistently recurring evidence of the era, thanks to the recycling of television and related technologies—the unemployed, if they were revealed at all, were cast as buffoons (the brothers Marx, the Three Stooges, and variations thereon), and their comedic misadventures pointed to the strong prospect of their utter unemployability, even in flush times. Most of the children of Our Gang seemed oblivious to the poverty in which they were mired, relishing instead the striking range of possibilities for innovation it offered to enterprising youngsters. The poor, in short, were usually hilarious; and if poverty could be treated so obliquely, so could a great many other issues. The ramifications of such notions as class distinction were confronted only indirectly, customarily through the genre of romantic comedy, a la Frank Capra. Otherwise, hard-boiled detectives and an array of oriental sleuths, singing cowboys, and gymnastic lords of the jungle, athletic interstellar heroes and high-stepping gold diggers, and a regular posse of man-made monsters, migrating vampires, and enormous apes carried the day. Such fanciful things were matinee fare at everyone's Bijou or Rialto; and they bore little relationship to the real world.[2]

And thus it was with the comics medium. Before 1929, newspaper strips and Sunday comic sections, important cultural transmitters since the turn of the century, were known as "funnies," a term implying humorous intent. Funnies offered slices of life, situation comedies of brief duration and generally domestic in their orientation. After 1929, however, they seemed something less than funny to increasing numbers of readers who failed to find amusing prospects in the framework of daily life. The world was in turmoil, the economy was in serious trouble, and the antics of assorted flappers, high rollers, and down-and-out immigrants could not relieve, even for the moment, the gloomy aspect of the rest of the newspaper. Hard times had blunted the appeal of the so-called funnies.

On January, 7, 1929, the adventures of "Tarzan" and "Buck Rogers" first appeared on newspaper comic pages, heralding the advent of what would become known as the "adventure strip." Following "Tarzan" in the 1930s were "Dick Tracy," "Jungle Jim," "The Phantom," "Terry and the Pirates," and dozens of others. All of them featured continuing stories, exotic locales and/or characters, virtually nonstop action, and little if any humor. They served to transport readers elsewhere—to a jungle, a desert, the Far East, a distant planet, or some other atypical environment where heroes struggled against tall odds or fabulous creatures, and where nothing had any real bearing on the problems of the day. As the decade progressed, adventure strips grew in popularity, fueling escapist fantasies for the economically distressed.[3] Because comic books developed from comic strips, they reflected the same shifting emphases.

The comic book emerged as a discrete medium of American cultural expression early in the 1930s. In its initial form, it contained only reprints of newspaper comic strips and was offered by publishers in bulk to companies in search of premiums and giveaways to increase their sales of everything from breakfast cereal to children's shoes. So popular was the comic book in this entrepreneurial venue that some publishers were led to believe it could be marketed directly to youngsters through news dealers, drugstores, and other retail outlets for a dime per copy. Early comic books—*Funnies on Parade* (1933) and *Famous Funnies* (1934) were two of the first—bore titles that belied the newspaper trend toward adventure comics, although they did reprint some of the post-1929 adventure strips.[4] But by the end of the decade, such publications as *Detective Comics* (1937) and *Super Comics* (1938) bespoke a significant thematic change, as comic books began to offer more and more original material prepared specifically for the new medium. These items were among the precursors of the vaunted "golden age" of comic books, which began during the summer of 1938 with the debut of Superman in the first issue of *Action Comics*.[5]

The impact of the Superman character upon the subsequent development of the comic book would be difficult to overestimate. Here was a seemingly human being who possessed a number of superhuman powers, a costumed hero with a secret identity, an alien from a dying planet who embraced American ideals and Judeo-Christian values—a kind of spectacular immigrant, as it were, come from afar to participate in the American dream. He had speed and strength and was invulnerable to manmade weaponry. He could not fly, but he could jump well enough to sustain the illusion. He was the nemesis of criminals, extracting confessions of their misdeeds by displaying his awesome powers; but, withal, he did not kill, or at least not more than was absolutely necessary—and there was an index of his healthy psyche and wholesome persona.[6] As a cultural artifact, Superman gained an enormous audience in fairly short order, passed from comic books into a variety of media including animated cartoons and radio, and endured in his basic format, though further translated by television and motion pictures, for half a century.[7] If imitation is, as Charles Caleb Colton said, the most sincere flattery, then Superman was the most flattered of all comic-book creations, spawning a host of look-alike, act-alike costumed heroes, all owing their existence to the norms and conventions his character established.

The appearance of Batman in the May 1939 issue of *Detective Comics* marked the emergence of another kind of heroic prototype. In this instance, a man of means (he had millions), when summoned by police, donned a bizarre costume (intended both to conceal his real identity and to terrify crooks) and swung into action (literally on the end of a rope, in most cases, even though the other end of it did not appear to be attached to anything). Batman possessed no superhuman powers. The skills he offered in behalf of law and order were merely those of the superior athlete and the brilliant scientist, and that was probably as close to reality as the story line came—which is to say that it missed by quite some distance. Like their adversary, Batman's criminal opponents were peculiar characters, altogether unusual in appearance and demeanor; and they contributed much to the surreal, nearly gothic aura of the Batman comic books.

Batman, too, was widely imitated, especially after the appearance of Robin as his adolescent sidekick in the April 1940 issue of *Detective Comics*. Within a matter of weeks, the duo appeared in the first issue of *Batman Comics*. Batman and Robin established the comic-book precedent for heroic partnerships between grown men and young boys, and their success made such pairings very nearly *de rigueur* in the medium during the 1940s. Here, after all, was a telling point of identification for an eager juvenile readership with dimes to spend.

Superman, Batman, and their numerous cultural clones were wholly fantastic constructs, in keeping with the escapist thrust of Depression-era popular culture. Arguably, they owed much to the renditions of other media. If, for example, radio's Lone Ranger and Tonto (no kid, granted, but clearly possessed of limited talents and abilities and thus kidlike) had been demonstrating since 1933 that a hero and a half were better than one, Batman and Robin merely offered further evidence.

And if audiences appreciated the costumed flummery of, say, Buster Crabbe's Flash Gordon movie serials, then perhaps Superman succeeded no less from a growing general interest in science fiction as an entertainment genre than from his exhibition of hybrid qualities revealed onscreen by Flash's friends as well as his enemies—strong men with wings, and all of that. But comic books could carry heroes beyond the limits of possibility imposed by radio (sounds without pictures and thus without depth or significant personification) and film (sounds with pictures, but constrained by technology). Radio, short on data, gave the consumer's imagination too much latitude, while film, rife with data, refused to give it enough. Comic books, however accidentally, managed to split the difference. They could show whatever the artist could draw, their lines and colors directing imagination, their balloon-held texts defining time and space. Comic-book artists and writers could produce that which could be conceived, which was more than the creators of motion pictures and radio programs could claim. Moreover, comic books escaped consideration according to aesthetic criteria established by adults for the evaluation of media offerings intended for the grown-up world. They were for children, and they enjoyed a certain freedom.[8]

As the 1940s began, comic books were being published in larger and larger quantities, and new characters were appearing every month. Heroes proliferated. The Green Lantern, Captain Marvel, and the Atom led the parade in 1940—respectively, an ordinary mortal endowed with alien powers, a boy who could become a man at will, and an extremely small fellow to whom size, or rather his lack of it, was no handicap in a world of frequently malicious larger folk. By 1941, The Justice Society of America had made its appearance as the first consortium of comic-book heroes: Green Lantern, the Atom, the Flash, Hawkman, Hourman, Sandman, the Spectre, and

Dr. Fate collaborated against criminals in a continuing alliance, a unique association that would establish yet another trend within the comic-book industry. Captain America, Plastic Man, Daredevil, and Fighting Yank were among the other heroes who first appeared in 1941. Their very names revealed their unreality.

The presence of so many colorfully-clad strongmen in comic books suggested to some observers that young female readers were being ignored. The masked and caped crime fighters seemed ideally structured to serve as role models for boys, so why should there not be a corresponding model for girls? In response, psychologist William Moulton Marston, in collaboration with artist Harry G. Peter, developed a costumed heroine he named Wonder Woman. She first appeared in the November 1941 issue of *All-Star Comics* as yet another prototype, albeit one who lived for years in the shadow of the male protagonists.

All these new heroes had plenty besides crime with which to contend, since, by 1940, war raged in Europe and Japanese militarists were having their way in the Far East. International politics had replaced economics as the major public preoccupation in the United States, and comic-book publishers, seeing fresh opportunities, began paying editorial attention to the real world for the first time. Their heroes, who had been unable to grapple with the complex issues of the Depression, could now set sights on the political arena, at first fighting fascism as a form of international crime in a limited involvement that came several months before America's entry into World War II.[9]

It may have been an appropriate cultural response in the context of the time, given the burgeoning nationalism of the Axis powers; but in any case, impelled by world affairs and the public mood, the comic-book industry fashioned a number of patriotic heroes for popular consumption. These included Fighting Yank, descendent of a Revolutionary War soldier who received his powers from that long-dead ancestor; Captain America, a chemically enhanced human being created by the military as the first member of a proposed army of supersoldiers; and perhaps the most peculiar—and peculiarly American—hero of all, Uncle Sam, who first appeared in the aptly named *National Comics* in July 1940. Once these and other such characters were in place, it was a relatively simple matter to match them against Axis villains, anticipating the day when the United States surely would have to join the conflict in an official capacity.

Many in the comic-book industry seemed to believe that American involvement in the war was inevitable. The attitude led to intense speculation and some rather loud rattling of cultural sabers. In that regard, it was less surprising than it might now seem that the eighteenth issue of *National Comics*, on newsstands early in November 1941, depicted the Japanese attack on Pearl Harbor that would not happen until a month later. Viewed in retrospect, the comic book's striking cover does not suggest the prescience of the medium; rather it indicates that when a single medium explores enough dramatic possibilities proceeding from a given set of circumstances, one or two such explorations are likely to be right on the money. It was simply that a year and a half of guessing on the part of *National Comics* staff had paid expected dividends, since from the perspective of comic books American participation was a foregone conclusion.

If rumors of war hinted at the end of escapism in American comic books, the fact of war presented empirical evidence of it. The questions at hand concerned national survival and the ability of the individual American to cope with the inevitable stress of awaiting an outcome. Comic-book heroes had new roles to play. Whereas crime fighting may have qualified as escapist fare during the 1930s (to the extent that crime was not a thing that touched every life), war was a different matter. Even the Depression had not affected the entire population, which may help to explain why popular culture could have afforded to ignore it. Moreover, crime had been the dilemma of local, state, and federal agencies, and the Depression had been widely viewed as a problem depending upon national political leadership for satisfactory resolution. In contrast, war concerned all Americans, and the cooperation of all would be required to insure a successful conclusion. It was not, as a rule, a time for cultural fun.[10]

Comic books brought much to the American cause. In addition to lending support to such necessary activities as bond drives and paper drives, comic books became an integral part of the Allied propaganda machine, emphasizing the need for a maximum war effort by portraying the enemy as the inhuman offspring of a vast and pernicious evil. Writers coined epithets like "ratzi" and "Japanazi," and artists drew rodentlike Japanese and bloated, sneering Germans. Japanese troops wore thick glasses and displayed prominent teeth, while German officers possessed monocles and dueling scars, much as they did in the wartime renditions of Hollywood filmmakers—although comic-book illustrators took greater liberties than Hollywood could, and to greater effect, given the nature of caricature. Comic books of the war years often bore dramatic covers—the full-color strangling of Hitler by a costumed hero, for example—which suggested an intensity of feeling but nevertheless frequently belied the contents of the issue. While the details of Hitler's agonized death might not (and probably would not) be recounted on the inside, comic-book heroes still could be relied upon to do something grand for the war effort and to wave the flag at regular intervals. Once the cover had stirred the blood, the slightest thing should serve well enough to keep it circulating, such books suggested.[11]

Once America entered the war, the prevalence of heroes with superhuman powers created problems for comic-book publishers. Were the United States to unleash these impervious patriots upon the Axis, the war could reasonably be expected to end in an hour or less. Some explanation of why that would not happen had to be forthcoming if the credibility, and ultimately the utility, of the heroes were to be maintained, even among unsophisticated juvenile audiences. Publishers responded according to the characteristics of their heroes. Some risked having their less-powerful creations travel abroad, where protracted struggle could indicate that the enemy was altogether tougher than anyone had expected and explain why the war would not end quickly.[12] Others allowed their heroes only indirect participation in the war, lest the plausibility of the characters be lost. On the one hand, Superman might indeed have asserted that "our boys" could handle the nasty business of war without his help; but on the other hand, it was also true that Superman's alter ego, Clark Kent, had managed to fail his preinduction physical, which had conveniently kept the "man of steel" from any involvement in a foreign theatre.[13] While Superman did eliminate the occasional spy or saboteur at home, he did not routinely have the chance to strangle Hitler. Nor did Captain Marvel, who also stayed home and fought saboteurs, although in one story his creators did opt for allegory, allowing their hero to encounter a pair of malevolent trolls who closely resembled the leaders of Germany and Italy. They, it seemed, were ruining the lives of the rest of the trolls, who were ordinary, though small and subterranean, folk desiring only a return to peace in their time.[14] And so forth and so on, in as many permutations and variations as there were costumed and powerful characters.

War stimulated the comic-book industry, not only by providing much of the editorial matter but also by expanding the audience for comic books. Hundreds of thousands of comic books were shipped to American service personnel around the world. True, the books were inexpensive and portable and thus logical fare for troops in transit; but, as well, they satisfied the requirement which dictates that popular culture appeal to the lowest common denominator, in this case the individual with limited language skills and the capacity to respond to only a narrow range of cultural symbols. The mobilization of a total of some 16 million Americans by war's end suggested a number of possibilities to comic-book publishers, and they made every effort to capitalize on them. The quality of their product was of no concern in that economic environment.[15]

Sending comic books to military personnel testified to the utility of the medium in raising morale through patriotic fervor, even if it should be achieved through appeals to racism. Laden as they were with unlikely heroic models, comic books could still inform about unity on the home front and indicate the extent to which American soldiers were glorified in a predominantly domestic medium. Even an illiterate could discern from comic books the virtue of the American cause and the sterling qualities of the American fighting man. Comic books served up a four-color version of a war in which the issues were black and white; they questioned nothing; and they dealt almost exclusively in happy—which is to say, victorious—endings. If this were indeed the "last good war," the comic books of the period bear witness to the accuracy of the label.

The war changed the appearance of comic books, probably because so many servicemen read them. By 1945, their artwork had developed a sexual orientation remarkable in a medium ostensibly still intended for juvenile audiences. A typical wartime cover might reveal in the foreground a scantily clad woman, tied with ropes or chains, at the mercy of some leering Axis villain, while in the background an American hero struggled forward, intent upon her rescue. The woman's clothing inevitably was torn to reveal ample cleavage and thigh, her muscular definition enhanced by forced contortion into some anatomically impossible position. Sometimes, her clothing was completely ripped away, leaving her to face her tormentor clad only in her unmentionables—which, presumably, gave added incentive to that struggling hero back there. The stories inside rarely if ever fulfilled the promises of such a cover, but they usually paid sufficient attention to female secondary sex characteristics to warrant a fellow's perusal.[16]

World War II may have ended in 1945, but in comic books it raged on for another year or two, until publishers had exhausted their backlogs of war-related stories. But by then, they had created a serious problem for themselves. By 1946 or 1947 readers, whether they were children or belonged to the older audience built by the war, were jaded by the redundant deeds of redundant heroes. The costumed types, pale copies of Superman and Batman to begin with, had exhausted the dramatic possibilities of the medium as well as of their individual personae by having done, in four action-packed years, everything that anyone could imagine them doing. By the end of the war, comic-book heroes had been pushed to all manner of improbable pastimes, including tearing Axis tanks in half and leaping from one aircraft to another in the middle of a dogfight. Such foolishness continued for awhile, thanks to those backlogs, but it was simply too much for readers to bear, and comic-book sales plummeted.[17]

Once the backlogs were exhausted, heroes had to return to crime fighting to make their contributions to society—and thus to earn their keep, for what good is a hero who does not practice his trade? But in the wake of a world war, that was nothing if not anti-climactic. Any number of heroes fell by the way, unable to pull their weight on an issue-to-issue basis. The survivors retained a loyal following, but a small one by comparison to what once had been. The very survival of comic books may well have been problematical in the minds of some publishers after 1945.

But of course the medium did survive, and it did so by adapting to a new socio-cultural climate with a radically different psychological construct. The war had brought current affairs into the comic pages, and there could scarcely be retreat from that, owing to the circumstances of war's end. Hiroshima and Nagasaki had rather emphatically illustrated the futility of the kind of escapist fantasy prevalent before 1940. Comic books, like other entertainment media, could not ignore what the world had become, nor could they effect a return to simpler times. Who needed a superman when we, with our atomic bombs, had become supermen? Comic-book publishers were willing to change, to adjust their focus, because they supposed that there was plenty of money still to be made. But first, they had to relearn their constituency. Like most other Americans, they had to discover what the nation had become, in consequence of victory.

2
The Bomb

By dropping atomic bombs to force a Japanese surrender in 1945, the government of the United States brought the American people to the brink of a moral crisis the likes of which they had not known since the issue of slavery had divided the nation three-quarters of a century before. The utter destruction of Hiroshima and Nagasaki had shortened the war—or so the government's, and particularly Harry S. Truman's, argument ran—and had saved thousands of American lives that might have been lost in a final assault on the Japanese home islands. Those were assertions of questionable validity, and they have been debated ever since; but what was unexpected in 1945 was the somber disapprobation of the community of nations. America, formerly righteous (and frequently self-righteous), had abdicated its position of moral leadership by employing the tactics of its enemies, namely the mass obliteration bombing of civilian populations. It had lowered itself to the level of the worst enemies of mankind as revealed by the bloody page of history. Never mind that it had been a just war against the perpetrators of the Holocaust and other heinous crimes. What seemed to count at the end was that American scientists had developed the most horrible weapon anybody had ever seen, and that the United States had used it, not once but twice. And no apologies were forthcoming—certainly not from Harry S. Truman. For the rest of the world, which did not love us as we loved ourselves, that was a disturbing turn of events.[1]

Bureaucratic justification of enormous acts of destruction is one thing, but cultural acceptance of them is something else altogether. Since culture functions to systemize values and has an internal orientation—which is to say that American culture first serves Americans, no matter who else may be affected by it, then or later—normalization of the abnormal is an inevitable consequence, whether the abnormality in question is a talking mouse, a strange visitor from another planet, or an atomic bomb. In the case of the Bomb (as it came to be known), Americans had an instant star for their various media; and, early on, the process of normalization began.

There was a period of adjustment, of course. It took some time for the news to sink in, some time for people to try to grasp exactly what had happened. Two large cities may not be leveled in such dramatic fashion and at such a staggering cost in human lives without some contemplation of the act and its meaning. But here Americans proceeded from a position of ignorance. They possessed little or no useful information. Had the scientists really known what they were doing? Had the president known what he was doing? It seemed reasonable and altogether patriotic to assume so. Besides, the Japanese had been the enemy and, more than that, thoroughly despicable people, according to four years' worth of propaganda. They had expressed violent contempt for white people, and they had been intent upon world domination. What if they had won? Where would America be then? In view of the even more dreadful alternative, Americans could not manage to be very sorry about what had happened at Hiroshima and Nagasaki—at least not at first.

In the flush of victory, some Americans saw the Bomb as confirmation of several of the ethnocentric notions long dear to the popular mind. The Bomb was clear evidence that God was on our side: His gift of the Bomb ranked right up there with the one involving His only begotten Son. That the principal recipient of such largess should be the leading Christian nation on the face of the earth did not escape the notice of

15

right-thinking Americans. But, too, the Bomb underscored popular perceptions of enduring and unbeatable American know-how and emphasized the superiority of American science and technology to a world now backward in comparison to the United States. The cultural hoopla surrounding the Bomb at once suggested cosmic beneficence and conveyed the image of an American Jack Horner who, having stuck his thumb into what amounted to Nature's pie, had produced one hell of a thing and was busily congratulating himself about it.[2]

The celebration was relatively short-lived. By 1946 we had located our conscience.[3] And by 1949, the Russians had a bomb of their own. The public developed a bad case of nerves thereafter. The gnawing question was, if we had possessed the Bomb and we had used it, what would keep our enemies from doing unto us in similar fashion? We had known when to use it, or so we liked to think, and why—but could a godless Communist be relied upon to behave as responsibly as we had? Thanks to our new views of our former wartime allies, the Russians, few doubted that the answer was uncompromisingly negative. There was a new reality, and culture had to make some adjustments. It had to make that new reality bearable.

Through the 1950s, media, with the inspiration of government, preached the survivability of atomic war. One might have some problems at ground zero, but farther away, one needed only a bit of shelter, some food and water, and a willingness to follow instructions in order to make it safely through an atomic bombing. Fallout was at best a minor concern, and government would be there afterwards to make sure that chaos did not reign. There was considerable nonsense in those early pronouncements, but so great was public discomfort that the silliest of precautions could be solemnly recommended and gladly embraced. They relieved anxiety for the moment by stressing the power of the individual to do something for himself and his loved ones in the face of prospects for utter destruction.[4]

What developed in the late 1940s, then, was a rather curious variety of folklore—a mythic vision of the Bomb, intended to accommodate the thing to everyday life, to make it an unobtrusive engine of death, so to speak. The comic-book contribution to the folklore centered on advancing the idea of a benign Bomb, a friendly Bomb, a Bomb that would never hurt anybody unless we willed it—and certainly it would never hurt us.

In comic books intended for young children, the Bomb might serve as a means of transportation from one venue to another, so that a character wishing to visit a place like Greenland or some other exotic locale had only to sit upon the device, await the explosion, and travel to his or her destination with the utmost dispatch and in perfect safety.[5] In such renditions, the Bomb became merely another item available to the slapstick comedian, sharing with cream pies and rubber hammers the qualities of being uproariously funny and ultimately harmless. Beyond that, use of the Bomb in comic-book advertising reinforced the idea that atomic explosions could mean fun for kids. In 1951, for example, Fawcett Publications arranged the titles in its line of comic books around a rather emphatic drawing of a mushroom cloud in a house advertisement of "Adventure for the Atomic Age" that linked the likes of Tom Mix, Gabby Hayes, and Tex Ritter with a thoroughly different kind of image.[6]

Although comic books for older readers carried discussions of the Bomb in other directions and spoke of death and destruction in consequence of atomic blasts, they nevertheless managed to portray a weapon consistently friendly to Americans. The message seemed to be that our atomic devices could kill our enemies, but their atomic devices could not harm us. If that was a curious interpretation of physical laws, it was also a variation on an older theme in popular entertainments, according to which bad guys and good guys might possess identical technologies—by Colt or Winchester, say—but the good guys would triumph because they were more competent in the application of those technologies.

Atom-Age Combat, a comic book published in 1952 and 1953 (by which time the United States possessed the hydrogen bomb), advanced such notions in a series of stories about Captain Buck Vinson, an officer in the Atlantic Commandos, an American outfit battling Russians and Chinese in an ongoing atomic war with theatres all over the world. Vinson and his men were armed with atomic artillery, atomic grenades, atomic rifles that fired atomic bullets—in short, atomic everything. Thus could they kill a great many Communists. Those Russians and Chinese, however, seemed able only to tear up the landscape, despite the fact that they were similarly armed. In one episode, the Atlantic Commandos were dispatched to Africa to take control of a new uranium deposit, since both sides in what was billed as the "War of Wars" were running out of the stuff, and they needed it to continue producing all that atomic ammunition.[7] The mission brought Vinson and his men into a showdown with Air Marshal Boris "The Butcher" Kasilov, a Russian in command of an army of "Red Asians" who had captured the uranium mine in a sneak attack. By and by, Vinson and the local Allied military attaché met Kasilov in the jungle. "Take cover," Vinson shouted to his companion. "He's going to toss a hydrogen grenade!" And this the Butcher did—from a distance of about ten feet. There was a terrific explosion, but, as the narration explained, "a massive tree trunk shielded the pair from the radioactive blast." Nor was Kasilov injured. Instead, he died when a passing gorilla seized him and broke his neck. It was, Vinson observed, almost as if the gorilla "knew the Allied forces deplore destruction of wildlife."

Here, then, were smart weapons indeed, excepting Americans, their allies, and assorted fauna from any serious atomic consequences. The story suggested that our Bomb was somehow in harmony with Nature, which was itself a politically partisan entity that knew enough to crush Soviet vertebrae and protect Americans from enemy radiation, because we were on Nature's side. Less ambiguously, the story expressed the philosophy inherent in comic books like *Atom-Age Combat*, which was that wars were necessary, good guys never died, and the Bomb was acceptable as a tactical weapon.[8] Some other comic books, however, were considerably more pessimistic.

The first issue of *Atomic War!*, dated November 1952, bore a cover depicting the destruction of New York City and offered a three-part story (set in 1960) that began with a Russian sneak attack on the United States, proceeded to the Russian invasion of Western Europe, and concluded with the launching of a retaliatory strike on the Soviet Union from a secret American bomber base in Greenland.[9] According to the story line, the Russians were bald-faced liars who, through wicked Commie guile, managed a reprise of Pearl Harbor, albeit on a much larger scale; and for this they would have to pay dearly, since one may not destroy America simply by blowing up a number of major cities and killing a few million people. The comic book asserted that any who responded positively to Soviet overtures about peace or anything like that were guilty of monumental stupidity that bordered upon treason. The oft-repeated message that "only a strong America can avert World War III" seemed to be aimed at any potential Neville Chamberlains in the federal government who might happen across a copy of the comic at the Capitol newsstand. After all, Russians had spoken of peace but then had bombed New York, Chicago, and Detroit, and that was what appeasement got you. Furthermore, there was evidence in this tale that Soviet leaders lied to their own people as well as to the Americans. Captured Russian pilots said they had been told by their high command that the United States planned a sneak attack, thus making a Soviet first-strike absolutely necessary.

The stories in *Atomic War!* were sandwiched between advertisements for U.S. Savings Bonds ("it's *practical* as well as patriotic to buy bonds for defense"), in keeping with the positive, remarkably upbeat attitudes exhibited by the characters in those stories, even in the face of atomic holocaust. More surprising, in the sense that it contradicted some of the enthusiasm for an atomic exchange expressed throughout the book, was a blurb appearing on the last page, beneath the heading "Win Cash Prizes!": "This magazine was meant to shock you—to wake up Americans to the dangers, the horror and utter futility of WAR! Write us—tell us how well we've succeeded, and the best letters will win valuable cash prizes!"

The utter futility of war had not been mentioned theretofore—indeed, quite the contrary—but the idea of winning fifteen dollars by discussing it in one hundred and fifty words or less was nicely suited to the absurdist context of the entire venture. If one is to take up the study of the end of the world, it is well to make a little money from it, inasmuch as Americans knew beforehand that most of them would survive.

Some comic-book creators chose to examine, not what the Communists might do with the Bomb, but what international criminals surely would do with it, if they should happen to become privy to American secrets. Here were pitches for world peace, preachments on a cosmic level, wherein American heroes saved the day and passed judgment on the human condition. When, for example, Wonder Woman thwarted the plans of Master De Stroyer, who had stolen an "atomic engine" from the United States in order to manufacture enough bombs to bring the world to its knees (he was, of course, eventually blown to smithereens by his own devices), she could observe, "Those who live by violence are more than likely to meet a violent end!"[10]

If that explained nothing about the justifications for American proprietorship of the Bomb vis-à-vis what we shall hereafter call the Red Menace, it did have something to say about human behavior, and that explained a great deal. America had developed and retained the Bomb because the behaviors of some other people were suspect. But neither Wonder Woman nor any other comic-book survivor of World War II could come around to advocating its use, since a second employment of such a horrible weapon would weaken our moral posture and set us up to . . . well, "meet a violent end." It was altogether a better idea to control the Bomb by controlling ourselves, and to control others by controlling their access to the Bomb. If that had not worked out exactly as it should have—and now we speak of real life—it did not mean that we should not keep trying. Perhaps the solution in the 1950s was to build a bigger, better Bomb, and to work doubly hard to keep this one under wraps. Master De Stroyer, after all, had settled for filching the atomic engine only after he had been told by minions that stealing the secrets of the hydrogen bomb was "impossible."

There was a degree of internationalism in comic-book consideration of the Bomb; and the ultimate internationalist was probably Captain Marvel, who favored world peace and the United Nations, in approximately that order. In the October

1952 issue of *Whiz Comics*, the good Captain, ever one to participate at the level of allegory, took off for the South American jungle, where highly intelligent orders of ants and wasps were waging atomic war over the question of which species would control the world.[11] The ants had stolen atomic secrets from American defense plants without difficulty (they were small enough to pass through security systems undetected), and the wasps had stolen from the ants. When Captain Marvel encountered the ant warlord, this exchange occurred:

> *Marvel (strangling the ant)*: You heartless wretch! War is stupid in the first place! Why can't you insects live together in peace?
> *Warlord*: Let go of me! Why can't *you humans* live together in peace? Who are you to preach?
> *Marvel (dropping the ant [PLOP!] and flying away to negotiate with the wasps)*: Er—he's got something there! But still, we're striving to keep peace with the UN!

As alter ego Billy Batson, Marvel persuaded the wasp warlord to reveal the location of his atomic plant by offering him the secret of the more powerful hydrogen bomb. Once inside the plant and after a couple of minor problems, Batson became Marvel again, heaved the wasp warlord into his own atomic pile, and created a chain reaction that blew up everybody's stash of atomic bombs. ("Impervious to any death-dealing weapon," the narration assured, "Captain Marvel survives the explosion!") Before returning north, Marvel convinced the surviving ants and wasps to form the UI—for United Insects. "Like our United Nations," he said, "it will promote peace here in your insect civilization!"

Anything to give hope—a viable United Nations, a new bomb better than the old Bomb, a minimally dangerous (now that it was in enemy hands) old Bomb—constituted the comic-book response to the unthinkable, a response which in itself indicated the extent to which lots of people were indeed thinking about the unthinkable. Yet in all of these constructs, culture also argued that the ultimate madness was not that at all. The Bomb was ours because we had made it, and those who stole it could never understand it as well as we did. Besides, we could always top it with a more terrible device whenever we pleased. We would survive because it was our Bomb, and, no matter what, it was friendly. Here was an indication of deep and abiding faith in American science and technology, based on the hearsay of history, the promotions of journalism, and the splendors available in the world's foremost consumer culture.[12]

It is worth noting that the Japanese had a different view and went on to develop a substantial popular culture based upon it, beginning in the late 1950s. In a succession of Japanese science-fiction films, monsters of horrific destructive potential stomped through cities, flattening buildings and stampeding the citizenry, all in consequence of having been awakened from centuries-long sleep by vibrations from atom-bomb tests. Resolution of the particular crisis could not be effected through either science or technology. The schemes of scientists always came to nothing, and military hardware proved useless. In the end, and for reasons beyond human understanding (there were sometimes hints of the supernatural), the monsters simply went away. The message of these films harked back to 1930s classics of the genre, notably *Frankenstein*. Mess with Nature, the films asserted, and what happens will not be pleasant to experience. Whether they accepted the argument or merely admired the special effects, Americans embraced the films, which enjoyed great popularity in the United States, beginning about 1956.[13] Clearly, they were aimed at Americans, a people who had surely messed with Nature and, with their testing of more and bigger bombs, continued to do so.

The Japanese, of course, knew how it felt to be powerless. Americans did not know and could not begin to imagine, although they had a better idea after 1949 than they had ever had before. There was evidence of malaise in postwar America—the divorce rate skyrocketed in 1946, for example, and in conjunction with social ills like juvenile delinquency, it led to a good deal of fretting about the future of the family, that most stable American institution. One can well imagine that even minimal concern about life with the Bomb added an unhappy aspect to the contemplation of a badly torn social fabric.[14] Culture could give children heroes to whom atomic explosions were as mosquito bites, and to whom radiation was as sunshine; but what could it provide in the way of comfort for older audiences? For all their faith in science and technology, the comic books could only teach small lessons of hope and imagination; and in the long run, they amounted to reinforcement for the pure of heart who would never have dared to challenge federal wisdom on any point as sensitive as the national defense.[15] There were some questions asked by comic books—difficult questions about the cost of our Bomb to the Japanese, for example—but they were infrequent, because, on the whole, American culture simply refused to make the Bomb an unhappy, unpleasant, or unappealing thing.[16]

On the Bomb's page in America's moral ledger, the debit side might have been full to overflowing, but it could not overbalance the credit side, even though that bore only a couple of entries. First, the Bomb had allowed the United States to win a just war against evil nations. Second, the Bomb promised to make war obsolete. Both meant the preservation of American lives. The first was verifiably so, according to the average American, an accomplished fact confirmed by history. The second was speculation, but it seemed reasonable.

Or it had, until the Russians obtained our secrets. And after that, Korea happened.

From *Atom-Age Combat* 1:3 (St. John Publishing Company: November 1952).

24

THE ROAR OF THE JETS AND ROCKETS HAS THROWN THE BEASTS INTO A MAD PANIC!

NOISE ALL GONE NOW. BAD SIGN!

YES, I'M AFRAID THE REDS HAVE CAPTURED OUR ANTI-AIRCRAFT DEFENSES. NOW TO FIND OUT IF THEY INTEND TO HOLD THE MINE OR DESTROY IT!

DEATHLY SILENCE HAD FALLEN ON THE CONGO WHEN MAJOR CORVELL REACHED AN OBSERVATION POINT...

THE REDS HAVE KILLED OR CAPTURED ALL BUT A FEW OF US WHO MAY HAVE ESCAPED, BUT THEY DAMAGED NONE OF THE MINING EQUIPMENT!

THEIR FIRST AERIAL ROCKET BARRAGE STRUCK OUR RADIO SHACK. THEY'LL DIG IN TO RESIST A COUNTER BLOW BEFORE I CAN RELAY THE NEWS TO ALLIED HEADQUARTERS.

SETTLE- MENT THREE DAY MARCH, MAJOR!

DEFYING JUNGLE PERILS, THE TWO MEN REACHED THE CONGO SETTLEMENT ON THE EVENING OF THE THIRD DAY...

THE LAST DOT-DASH OF THE CONGO SETTLEMENT TRANSMITTER HAD SCARCELY CLEARED THE ETHER WHEN A HUGE JET FLYING BOAT WAS ORDERED TO TAKE OFF FROM A SECRET ATLANTIC BASE!

28

29

30

DON'T THROW A ROCKET IN THERE. WE'LL TAKE HIM ALIVE, CAPTAIN.

OKAY, MAJOR!

WHILE COMMANDOS AND MINERS JOINED FORCES TO SCOURGE THE MINE AREA AND SURROUNDING JUNGLE OF THE RED INVADERS, BUCK VINSON AND THE BELGIAN MAJOR BEGAN A GRIM HUNT FOR MARSHAL KASILOV!

WE'LL HAVE THE MOST-WANTED WAR CRIMINAL ON EARTH IF WE CAPTURE HIM, CAPTAIN!

TAKING HIM ALIVE WILL BE A TERRIFIC BLOW TO ENEMY MORALE.

A SECRET ESCAPE HATCH THROUGH THE CAVERN ROOF! KASILOV SLIPPED OUT TO ESCAPE INTO THE JUNGLE!

YES, CAPTAIN, BUT HE MAY BE HIDING ABOVE UNTIL HE'S SURE OUR SIDE IS WINNING THE BATTLE.

THERE HE GOES, MAJOR! CAREFUL NOW! HE'S ARMED!

I KNOW EVERY INCH OF THIS JUNGLE. SOONER OR LATER HE WILL TRAP HIMSELF!

THE SHREWD BUTCHER SENSED THAT HIS IMMEDIATE DANGER LAY AHEAD, AND THAT HIS PURSUERS WERE NO THREAT AGAINST HIS LIFE.

BUT AS THE CHASE LENGTHENED, THE BUTCHER'S TEMPER GREW SHORT. TRAPPED IN A THICKET OF THORNS, HE SNORTED AT BUCK'S COMMAND TO DROP HIS WEAPON!

I'D SHOOT MYSELF RATHER THAN SURRENDER TO YOU DOGS!

TAKE COVER! HE'S GOING TO TOSS A HYDROGEN GRENADE!

33

3

The Red Menace

The structure of *story*, regardless of the medium through which it is told, requires some sort of conflict, and conflict requires some sort of resolution. As a matter of convenience, a reliable enemy is a fine thing for a storyteller to have. Artists, writers, and editors who earned their livings in the comic-book industry thus possessed ample reason to mourn the passing of the Axis leaders and their minions, having nothing handy to take their place except home-grown villains of the prewar years who were mild characters by comparison. Their criminal activities suggested nothing grand, no issue to inflame the imagination, nothing worth getting all stirred up about.

Some comic-book publishers tried to add zest by resurrecting the Third Reich—or was it the Fourth?—anticipating by at least three decades the preoccupation of other media with freeze-dried Nazis and Dr. Mengele's boys from Brazil. This was not the stuff of editorial backlog from the war years. Rather, it was material consciously generated to maintain a viable enemy at center stage, to keep a real war going, to blow a bit upon the patriotic spark. Was Hitler alive and well, hatching plans for world conquest from an underground city beneath Yellowstone National Park? Was the question worth asking, even in a comic book?[1] One imagines public apathy reaching monumental proportions. Clearly, new kinds of enemies were needed—enemies mysterious and menacing, and whose appearance on the scene conveyed some sense of urgency to consumers of popular culture. In other words, the public deserved the sort of lasting malevolence to which it had become accustomed during World War II.

And then came the Communists, who seemed to fill the bill rather nicely from a storyteller's standpoint. They might not have been enlisted except for their own efforts, which, by 1947, were prodigious and thus worthy of extensive reportage. The relevant chronology included the enunciation of the Truman Doctrine aligning the United States against Communist terrorism in Turkey and Greece in the spring of 1947; the Soviet blockade of Berlin the spring of 1948; the creation of NATO in August of 1949 to curb Russian expansionism; the severing of relations with Communist China in January 1950; and the commitment of American troops to Korea in June 1950. The Alger Hiss case, beginning late in 1948, the conviction in New York in October 1949 of eleven leaders of the American Communist Party for advocating the violent overthrow of the United States, and the trial of Julius and Ethel Rosenberg and Morton Sobell early in 1951 (we were missing a Bomb, remember) suggested the domestic aspect of international politics; and comic-book publishers had a Red Menace upon which to base their stories.[2]

The principal villains had to be the Russians, since they seemed particularly determined to be difficult. They had come to think of the destruction of Nazi Germany as the occasion for helping themselves to half of Europe. Joseph Stalin was, by most accounts, not a nice man. The Soviets had shown an inordinate interest in our atomic secrets, had tried hard to filch them, and had succeeded, with an operational Bomb of their own by 1949. We had to be alert to the possibilities of a fifth column. Red infiltrators could be anywhere. Anyone inclined to relax in the midst of these prospects had only to await the morning newspaper and the next screaming headline. Popular wisdom had it that the United States should have allowed Patton's armor to keep on rolling, through Germany and into Russia. Then the world would not have been locked in its current sorry condition. And so forth.

Into the 1950s, the daily news confirmed everyone's worst suspicions. In Korea, Russia's Red Chinese stooges revealed the brutality of which the Communist nations were capable. In Washington, Harry Truman seemed to have misplaced his spine on the question of vaporizing evil people with tidbits from our atomic arsenal, even though he had sufficient backbone for dealing with the policy-making aspirations of General Douglas MacArthur. Better to elect a general to the presidency outright, people said—and better a general like Dwight Eisenhower than the egghead offered by the Democrats in 1952, even though Ike was the one who stopped Patton. And if the fires of hysteria did not burn as brightly as they had during the Red Scare of the 1920s, they were fanned periodically by ambitious politicians who understood that virulent anti-Communism was a good platform from which to publicize themselves. What Texas congressman Martin Dies had begun with the House Committee on Un-American Activities in the 1930s emerged full-blown (if not grown) in the 1950s as the national spotlight focused on the likes of Wisconsin Senator Joseph McCarthy and Californian Richard Nixon, soon to be the general's vice-president. It was a time of seemingly rampant anti-intellectualism, perfectly suited, the cynic might say, to the expounding of comic-book philosophies.[3]

In keeping with their performance during World War II, popular media tried—though not always successfully, as we shall see later—to respond in positive, supportive fashion. Hollywood, itself under considerable fire for harboring writers, directors, and actors who were, if not bright Red, then at least shockingly pink, tended to exploit paranoia to pack 'em in at the box office. Its films depicted constant, unrelieved menace from enemies so anonymous that they could be the lady in the supermarket or the neighbor down the street. Fighting ubiquitous evil was no simple matter, such films as *I Was a Communist for the FBI* (1951) and *Big Jim McLain* (1952) seemed to suggest; and if movies of that ilk were not enough to keep the average American looking over his or her shoulder and into other people's business, the ones that delighted in revealing national vulnerability certainly were. These were allegorical treatments from the genre of science fiction (or maybe horror), wherein aliens from Mars or elsewhere were employed to represent the Red Menace. Cold, calculating, and utterly incapable of emotion (thus conforming nicely to popular ideas of what godless Commies were all about), these creatures were doubly dangerous: Not only did they argue for a mindless communalism too horrible to contemplate, they also were either (1) extremely difficult to kill with conventional weapons, or (2) extremely difficult to sort out of the general population, given their remarkable ability to look just like us. *The Thing from Another World* (1951) and *Invasion of the Body Snatchers* (1956) were prominent examples of Hollywood anti-Communism in the alien-invader, we'll-all-be-zombies mode.[4]

Comic books were considerably more optimistic, consistently assuming the swift and inevitable downfall of all Communist states, cells, and individuals. No need for paranoia from the comic-book perspective, given the legion of federal agents on the job to make the world safe for the American way. Comic books baldly stated that *our* people, being bigger, smarter, and tougher to start with, subdued *their* people every time.[5] At some point in virtually every story, American protagonists took to muttering the sort of hard-boiled political preachments that might have come from characters by Dashiell Hammett or Raymond Chandler, had they been counterspies instead of mere private detectives.[6]

In touting the heroics of Treasury Department agents, F.B.I. men, and operatives from various unnamed branches of government, comic books indicated acceptance of, and appreciation for, what might be called postwar pragmatism in dealing with Communists. American heroes, it seemed, were no longer required to play fair with their enemies. Rather, they fought fire with fire, in recognition of the dire consequences awaiting the free world if they should fail in any of their respective missions. Merely neutralizing Soviet agents—or, for that matter, Soviet armies—served no good purpose, given the stakes in the game; so homicide, and not infrequently genocide, became reasonable and acceptable undertakings for comic-book operatives. It all reflected a redefinition of societal standards, dating, no doubt, from the adoption by the United States of its enemies' tactics during World War II—again, that bombing of civilian populations. A nation that will assert the righteousness of its cause through those means can ill-afford to employ agents unprepared to acknowledge the efficaciousness of such approaches—or to employ them, should push come to shove. Theirs was not to reason why, simply because there was no need for intellectual rumination. And, sane people that they were, comic-book secret agents knew that it was better to kill a few Soviets, or a few hundred, or a few thousand, than to risk having Europe and the Americas overrun by Communist forces.[7] Presumably, it was also better than having to kill a few million Russians in an atomic war, although comic-book writers did not expound that philosophy in any certain terms, as we have seen.

If, on the one hand, comic books relied upon the implacable enmity of the Soviet regime in the early 1950s, they did, on the other hand, differentiate between the Russian people and their leaders. Here was a new courtesy, one scarcely extended to the German or Japanese populations during World War II. Russia had been an ally in the fight against Hitler, at least up to a point. Some comic books had gone so far as to lionize the Russian fighting man and woman, establishing them as worthy companions to the American soldier, and, on occasion, even as sidekicks.[8] Without that background, however, sympathy for the average Russian was still possible, owing to the prevalent perception of Communism as a political deal. According to the comic-book argument, the Russian Revolution had been a good and necessary thing, a movement of and by the people to liberate themselves from the yoke of Tsarist oppression. It may even have been comparable to the American Revolution in that regard. But, unhappily for the Russian people, their revolution was appropriated by a cruel, heartless group bent on the creation of a totalitarian state and capable, as it turned out, of violent excess far beyond any that the Tsar and his followers might have imagined. Thus, an otherwise virtuous revolution had resulted in the creation of a true police state and the emergence of Stalin's monstrous dictatorship; and the Russian people were, by the early 1950s, worse off than they had ever been before. As American comic books had it, Russia was a place where heavily armed soldiers waited in the underbrush to machine-gun hard-working peasants who dared to relate this forbidden history to their innocent children.[9]

American comic books interpreted the Chinese revolutionary experience in a somewhat different light. Dr. Sun Yat-sen, the revolutionary democratic nationalist, was the early hero; but he made the mistake of agreeing to accept Communist aid, and that brought in the Soviets, and there went the revolution—another popular movement usurped by the powers of political darkness. Hope for the future of a democratic China lay with Chiang Kai-shek's army on Formosa and its continuing efforts, with American support, to overthrow the Communists occupying the mainland.[10]

Such interpretations indicated that comic books were trying harder than ever before to inform American readers about the origins of current problems. One might easily debate the question of whether the data were intended to educate or to indoctrinate, but the significant point is that the data appeared at all. Here were explanations of world crisis a good deal more complex than those offered during World War II, perhaps reflecting the public perception that the world itself was a good deal more complex than it had been before 1945. Still, for all their weaving of tales about good revolutions subverted by bad people, comic books oversimplified for the sake of the argument no less than for the preferences of the market. Comic-book interpretations ignored vast swatches of inconvenient history, so that one did not have to consider, say, Chiang Kai-shek's education in Moscow and his massacres of Communist workers in northern China in the 1920s in juxtaposition to his status as democracy's Asiatic spokesman in the 1950s.

Inherent in the comic-book perspective on the Communist world was the notion that the enslaved masses of Russia, China, and assorted satellites ached to recapture their respective revolutions and cast out the agents of Soviet tyranny as the first order of business. Practically, such thinking tended to lower the odds against the comic-book spies and counterspies in the employ of the United States, indicating to the truly concerned reader that all a fellow really had to do was topple one or two members of the inner circle. Then, because one thing leads to another (as in the case of falling dominoes), the whole Communist bloc would crumble. Comic-book agents were not superheroes, and this sort of convention gave American protagonists an edge. It suggested that, at least on one level, the Cold War was a better conflict than World War II had been, to the extent that America's enemies were not fanatical populations but merely a few hundred fanatical individuals. It also suggested that most of the nations of the world could elude the Red Menace with just a little help from their American friends.[11]

Because American comic-book agents worked alone or in pairs—seldom were more than two ever required to thwart any Communist plot—the "domino" convention served to indicate the fragile underpinning of each subversive enterprise. American agents always aimed for the top man; and when he fell, of course, the whole plot collapsed. In this way, comic books stressed the superiority of American intellect by demonstrating the inferiority of the Communist mind. No matter how complex the Communist plan, and regardless of the amount of effort put into it, the comic-book agent had only to locate the proper domino and push.

Consider the September 1951 issue of *Kent Blake of the Secret Service*, wherein the protagonist parachuted into Tibet to learn why the Dalai Lama had begun "preaching a holy war against the western hemisphere."[12] In the bowels of the Pentagon, Agent Blake's boss had explained the urgency of the mission: "First there were stirrings of unrest. Now all of Asia is inflamed and awaiting his final word! If the Asiatic hordes are properly armed they could sweep over all of Asia, Europe, and Africa . . . then deal the death blow to our own civilization!"

Naturally, there had to be Communist influence behind anything as potentially devastating as that; and, sure enough, Blake learned that two Soviet agents had entered Tibet and murdered the Dalai Lama. One of them had assumed the holy man's identity and was in the process of inflaming the masses.

Blake, alone and in unfamiliar territory, managed to expose the plot, kill the two Soviet spies, and install the dead Dalai Lama's brother as the new spiritual leader. The tale ended with all the customary platitudes: America's flag would fly "high and proud" as long as the nation continued to produce men like Agent Blake, etc., etc. But Blake, for his part, shrugged off the whole adventure and took a nap.

American agents were at home anywhere in the world, it seemed, and coolly efficient, whatever their surroundings and regardless of their circumstances. Few were as casual as the sleepy Kent Blake, however. Clark Mason, for example, was an antipodal character, tough to the point of ruthlessness, and an utterer, not of platitudes, but of tight-lipped eulogies delivered over the corpses of his Communist foes. Even the presence of his frequent companion, a fetching female spy known as Vicki, could not soften his visage or demeanor as he dealt death to America's enemies. Of course, Mason often confronted more complicated situations than agents like Blake did, and so he enjoyed a smaller margin of error and had less fun.

In the November 1951 issue of *Spy Fighters*, Mason and Vicki entered Albania with orders to prove that refugees supposedly fleeing from Yugoslavia were fictitious creations of Soviet anti-Tito propaganda.[13] As it happened, the migration into Albania was genuine, but no refugees were crossing the border. Rather, the immigrants were Russian soldiers in mufti, assembling inside Albania and poised to strike at Europe. Mason foiled the plot by nailing the Russian officer in charge of the operation. The proper domino having been pushed, the entire plan failed, and the Russian was left to face music composed by his superiors at home. Spat Mason in conclusion, "There's only *one* refuge for a disgraced Commie! A little six by four territory where they *all* belong!"

Gutsy rhetoric aside, here were yarns with geo-political points of reference baffling to the adolescent and irrelevant to adults who read comic books for whatever visceral enjoyment might come from pictorial Red-bashing. *Foreign Affairs* it was not, but comic-book producers seemed to believe that the medium owed such accounts to its audience. The lengths to which artists and writers might go were suggested by a story concerning Communist activities in Kashmir in the April 1952 issue of *Spy Cases*.[14] It featured a map and a two-page introduction to the history of Hindu-Moslem relations in the region, as well as background on the long-standing conflict between India and Pakistan, which, of course, the Soviets wished to exploit, since a full-blown war between those nations would pave the way for a Communist takeover. Then and only then came Doug Grant, comic-book secret agent, to resolve matters involving a wealthy rug-merchant's secretly Communist daughter, a kidnapped American girl, and a yogi who had sat in cross-legged meditation in the mountains of Kashmir for twenty years without so much as a word to anyone until, upon observing Grant's struggle against overwhelming Communist odds, he hopped up to announce, "I will not stand by and watch liberty destroyed," and proceeded to save the American's life. It wanted a Sousa sound track and footnotes by George F. Kennan to round out the high drama in mountainous places; but, alas, it was only a story in a comic book, no more or less absurd than any other of its kind.

And therein lay the rub: Communists were having an easy time in the world, it seemed; and, no matter how great the desire of foreign peoples for peace and freedom, it always took an American to promote change.[15] Why were these people so completely unable to help themselves? They adored liberty, or so they said, and they outnumbered the Soviet agents who made their lives miserable. Why, then, could they not arise and slay the enemy as he slept? If comic books strived diligently for verisimilitude with maps and socio-political discourse, why was theirs a world so defiant of the logic inherent in the black-and-white values that had sustained the medium during World War II? Comic books appeared to have painted themselves into an unhappy corner with multiple shadings from a confused palette. They were too much of the world, and the world was no longer suited to the renditions of a popular art that had, for the moment, misplaced the lowest common denominator.[16] Comic books may have invented the friendly Bomb, but clearly that was not enough.

There is a bad old joke about a chameleon who sat upon

a patchwork quilt and experienced a nervous breakdown. From that imagery, however, one may discern the dilemma of the comic-book medium in post–World War II America. Comic books sought to mirror the real world for readers for whom mere escapism was no longer a satisfying indulgence. But the reflection they cast was disturbing in its implications and made escape seem somehow more desirable. Readers demanded a world they could understand, a world that corresponded to common sense. Thus, American spies like Clark Mason and Doug Grant left Tibet and Albania and Kashmir and went in uniform to the battleground of Korea, to serve as military intelligence officers in a simpler, less ambiguous theater of operations, where black and white were once again the dominant colors.[17] The ploy, however, resolved nothing except perhaps the publishers' problem: Korea, as it turned out, was not the stuff to salve the American psyche.

Meanwhile, there was the question of who would handle domestic Reds in the absence of federal counterspies. That work would be done, as we shall see in chapter 5, by people who had no business in Korea and consequently did not go.

From *Kent Blake of the Secret Service* 1:3 (20th Century Comic Corporation: September 1951). Battlefield: TM & © 1952 Marvel Entertainment Group, Inc. All rights reserved.

44

45

49

Kent Blake of the Secret Service: TM & © 1951 Marvel Entertainment Group, Inc.
All rights reserved.

50

4

Korea

As a unifying and uplifting cultural experience, the comic-book version of the Korean conflict left much to be desired. Here, seemingly, was a military adventure into which the true patriot could sink teeth: America and assorted United Nations allies in a showdown against the North Koreans (who were stooges of the Red Chinese, who were themselves stooges of the Soviet Union) over the fate of the plain, freedom-loving people of South Korea. And if it had to happen conventionally, without atomic weapons, it would be a mere walk-through for American troops, who, based on their performances against the Axis armies five years earlier, were undeniably the best in the world. But comic books could not always manage to portray a competent, loyal, and/or brave soldiery. They tried, to be sure; but in comparison to their accounts of World War II, what they presented about Korea was awash in ambiguity and uncertainty. They seemed obsessed by psychology, and they spoke constantly about death. Accordingly, in their treatment of Korea, they struck more than a few sour notes in what was supposed to have been a fairly simple tune of glory.

The early 1950s were a time when ambiguity, uncertainty, and psychology tainted a good many offerings from the mills of American popular culture. Comic books were but one affected medium. In Hollywood, even the western movie, a cinematic staple for the transmission of traditional American values since the 1920s, had succumbed to this postwar syndrome—and if westerns could be so violated, then nothing was safe. The movie image of gunslingers who talked more and fought less corresponded nicely to that of comic-book soldiers who struggled against their own neuroses as much as they did against their Communist enemies; but as a commentary on the American psyche, neither image could satisfy.

Certainly, comic books portrayed the American fighting man in a new and troubling light. He was frequently brave and sometimes cowardly, but whatever the quality of his courage, his character was probably not without serious flaw. In any case, he had a better than even chance to wind up dead. Never before had comic books discussed such matters so candidly.

To the extent that comic books mirrored society, they were treating, however elliptically, prevalent concerns over the condition of American males. One could not, in those days, articulate the notion that perhaps the Bomb had brought on a degree of psychological impotence by denying that final assault on Japan and lulling people into complacency with the idea that conventional war was a thing of the past, negating the long-held image of man-the-protector, man-the-hunter. But something had happened to American males, and nothing that was being said about men's roles or men's minds was particularly good news. In 1946, for example, Benjamin Spock had said that Mommy should raise the kids with minimal input from Daddy, so the kids would be well-adjusted. Two years later, however, the remarkably influential "Kinsey Report" revealed that more than a third of American males had participated in homosexual experiences, so maybe Mommy's historical influence was not a good thing. Harking back to the misogyny of Philip Wylie's *Generation of Vipers* and its attacks on "Momism," a new batch of critics blamed American women for rearing boys who were wimps, twits, and sissies. But they also blamed Dad for letting her do it. Maybe he had been off fighting a war. Maybe he was now off fighting another one. Maybe he was one of the homosexual third. Or maybe he was simply a creep—one of the 50 percent, according to the Kinsey research, who cheated on his wife. All this criticism, and poor Daddy was nevertheless expected by his country to go and meet the Reds in remote places and perhaps be killed. Even dead, he might be remembered as an ineffectual soldier.[1]

Death was the thing that separated comic books of the Korean era from those of World War II. In Korea, comic books held, American boys dropped like flies. Those who survived were confronted at every turn by irrefutable evidence of their mortality. One could not forget, even for a moment, the prospect of his own demise by bullet, bomb, grenade, artillery round, or, in the event of capture, torture at the hands of merciless, grinning Reds. There was so much death—and so much fear of it—in Korean-era comic books that it overwhelmed any and all jingoistic philosophies attendant upon individual stories. If that did not transform comic books into the only substantial body of public antiwar literature in the early 1950s, it surely dampened readers' enthusiasms for that kind of conflict. Moreover, the comic books were depicting a bloody war that readers knew from Bomb-related reportage was never supposed to have happened.[2]

Here, then, was a grim war in a bleak place where the terrain consisted largely of rocks.[3] Quite a few of our boys had brought their neuroses along. Those who possessed none were likely to find some among the rocks.[4] Even stable individuals were bound to succumb to psychological stress because our boys were often the victims of incompetent leadership, because they faced an enemy who was better armed and could demoralize, and because they had no very good idea why America had become involved in the conflict in the first place.[5] A surprising number of American troops were predisposed to desert or defect, and those who did not subscribe to notions like "better Red than dead" were still liable to capture and vulnerable to the brainwashing at which the Communists were rumored to be adept. Some American prisoners did not require psychological laundering. They sought to improve their circumstances through open collaboration with the enemy, and never mind that the Reds usually killed them.[6] In a three-year parade of comic-book pessimism, there seemed to be little room for the normal, sane, and healthy American soldier.

Portrayals of the enemy conformed in most cases to the Red-Menace imagery established elsewhere in the comic-book medium. Communist officers, be they North Korean, Chinese, or Russian, were always brutal and inhuman and, if they held any rank above major, usually stupid. They were subject to the domino principle from the spy comics, thanks to the fragile nature of Communist infrastructures no less than to the fact that these bullies spent nearly as much time and energy abusing their own men as they did harassing the Americans. Bragging about Communism and boasting of their genius, Red officers had great disdain for enlisted men, recruiting and sustaining them with lies and employing them tactically as cannon fodder, believing the whole time that these peasants (particularly if they were North Korean) were too ignorant to realize what was happening to them. Such officers, if strategic blunders did not bring them under American guns, were usually killed by their men, who always awakened to the truth sooner or later.[7] Indeed, every so often a Chinese or North Korean let it be known that he was a friend of the Americans, an individual who loved democracy, deplored Communism, and would gladly sacrifice himself to save American lives.[8]

Despite the occasional turncoat and whatever strife there may have been in the ranks, the Reds were not to be taken lightly. They were always capable of killing vast numbers of Americans, regardless of bungling leaders and unenthusiastic troops.[9] They had the capacity and predilection for atrocity, and, godless Commies that they were, no compunctions about committing it.[10] Therefore, it was necessary for Americans to remain alert at all times. Any momentary lapse could be fatal. In view of that, the comic books suggested, survival required the adoption of methods and manners characteristic of the enemy, which in practical terms meant that American soldiers had to become the unfeeling automatons they often criticized the Reds for being.[11]

Emotion was a luxury in which Americans ought not to indulge, because it could lead to psychological debility, if not to death. One might, for example, become attached to a lovable Korean orphan who subsequently died (probably from a Commie bullet), and then one would be vulnerable on account of a broken heart.[12] Common sense dictated that caring in the middle of a war was a monumental waste of time. Nor could one suppose that, because a Chinese had once lived in New York and had pictures of a pretty wife and cute kids to show, he could be anything other than an enemy who needed killing, despite the progress of friendship. A gook, after all, was a gook.[13]

The comic-book Reds were fully aware of each and every American weakness. Americans were not serious about war, were inclined too much toward moralizing, and were prone to permit too many distractions—all of which left openings for Communists to exploit. American traits provided opportunities for Red-wrought disaster. The average American soldier, for example, possessed a whopping and largely uncontrolled libido—not with regard to oriental women, necessarily, but show him a photograph of a white girl in revealing attire and, even if she were Russian, he was likely to moon over it for hours, carry it next to his heart for future reference, and forget all about where his mind was supposed to be in the meantime. If the Communists, recognizing that tendency, should happen to litter the front with pin-ups chemically treated to burst into flame in a matter of hours, they might reasonably expect to flash-fry several hundred American troops.[14] Soldiers would be well advised to recall the best top-kick instructions ("This is my rifle, this is my gun . . . ") from basic training and pay attention to business. If Communists could use sex to military advantage, there was no telling what else they might do.

How confused could one war be? Enemy leaders were cunning and dangerous but stupid. Enemy troops were victims of Communist duplicity but deadly. The Reds were better armed and equipped, but Americans were generally victorious. Americans were neurotic, but they were brave, except for the cowards (who were also neurotic), and many of the brave ones qualified as heroes; but everybody died for the most part, just the same.[15] There were bad good guys and good bad guys, and since a fellow knew not where he stood at any given time, it was well to be dispassionate to the point of heartlessness and unfeeling to the point of oblivion.[16] It was a fine idea, in short, to be a hard case—a state becoming to every God-fearing Christian American who confronted Communism, on or off the battlefield. But even so, the comic books, like the popular press in the early 1950s, could not avoid suggesting that there were too many sissies in this little war.[17]

As if the complex present were not enough with which to contend, war comics of the Korean era sometimes tackled history as well, offering revisionist perspectives of the previous war, or the one before that, or one several centuries in the past. A reprise of the fate of the Light Brigade in the Crimean War could provide the occasion for a preachment upon the follies of officers that resulted in young lives lost.[18] A retelling of Caesar's Gallic conquests could give rise to speculation on the possibility that the Roman chief, not Vercingetorix, had been the real barbarian, and that Caesar's assassination was in fact his reward for indulging in so much uncivilized behavior.[19] Between the same set of bright covers, one might find various tales that argued the brutal continuity of war, regardless of historical epoch. A story about a Korean orphan, one about Geronimo, one about Napoleon, and a retelling of the action at Anzio during World War II could all promote the assertion that war was "the same from year to year! The same viciousness, the same destruction, the same death!"[20]

One might find, as well, challenges to conventional wisdom concerning traditional American heroes. In the May–June 1952 issue of *Two-Fisted Tales*, for example, there was an enlisted man's version of the Battle of the Little Bighorn in which any number of atypical assertions appeared. Custer, according to the story line, was a peacock who cared nothing for the well-being of his men, inasmuch as he was willing to risk their lives to kill Indians for his own greater glory so that he might become president of the United States—and that was only the first page. By the second page, the trooper-narrator was asking God's forgiveness for the sinning he was about to do for Custer's sake. "We've got *no God-given right* to kill the poor redmen," he thought. "We've broken their treaties *again and again*! We've chased them out of their hunting grounds and killed their *women and children* . . . just so's Custer can get his glory!" By the battle's close, the soldier had enjoyed the spectacle of his commander's demise. "*Custer got us into this,*" he thought as he struggled on, badly wounded. "*Custer's to blame. He was the one who didn't want to wait for the rest of the Army . . . Ha! Custer's hit! He's killed! I'm glad! I'm glad!*" [21]

Perturbation of officers with the cowardice of enlisted men was the other side of the same coin, and the editors of *Two-Fisted Tales* chose to explore that topic in a story about George Washington in their September–October 1952 issue. The idealized Parson-Weems, father-of-his-country image had no place in this version of an early episode from the American Revolution. Seeing troops under his command desert en masse in the face of enemy fire, Washington first tried to rally the men (four panels), then turned to cursing them (four panels), then threatened to kill them (two panels). Nothing halted their headlong rush. The general, still on horseback but abandoned by his army and flanked by the British, became glazed, nearly comatose, "as if he were a man without his mind." The story ended with an oblivious Washington being led away by an aide, perhaps to fight another day, or perhaps not. [22]

Such revelations about certified American icons like Custer and Washington were probably subversive in the context of the times, regardless of editorial claims that the stories were based upon hours of research in places like the New York Public Library. [23] They were certainly antiwar pieces in the broader context of the times and the books in which they appeared, but it is questionable that they had much effect on children who happened to read them. What did bother the youngsters, and the thing to which they occasionally objected, was that so many of the war stories in *Two-Fisted Tales* had what they identified as "sad endings." Editors responded in defense of what they characterized as realism. [24] The remarks of older readers, many of whom were servicemen, seemed to indicate support for the portrayals of Korea in the war comics and were critical only with regard to specifics, such as incorrectly drawn military equipment. Among neither younger nor older readers did there appear to be any lessening of enthusiasm for the current conflict, despite incessant editorial harping about war's devastating effects upon individuals and society.[25]

Some comic books attempted to explore a lighter side of military life, with emphasis upon the Korean experience. There was a tradition here. The Sad Sack, a sort of enlisted everyman who had first appeared in newspaper strips during World War II, began a comic-book career in 1949, although he was initially a civilian during that incarnation. He reentered the army in the early 1950s, however, because the public found him to be a more appealing misfit in uniform. Likewise, Beetle Bailey began in a newspaper strip in 1950 and had made the transition to comic books by the late spring of 1953. The intent of both of these features was to lampoon army life without any particular reference to politics, foreign or domestic. Beetle Bailey, for example, never managed to leave Camp Swampy for Korea or anyplace else. Still, one could argue that the assaults these comics made upon such a prodigiously sacred American cow were, in and of themselves, political in nature, denigrating the military without a corresponding pitch for the war effort.

More appealing, especially to servicemen, were the comic books that displayed military high jinks in a decidedly patriotic context. Typically, these featured two soldiers who made a great show of disliking each other, frequently to the point of fisticuffs. Their differences were always minor and tended to involve a squabble over the affections of some comely lass—a nurse, a reporter, a visiting starlet or beauty queen, or perhaps even a fetching Communist spy—who happened to pass through the war zone. Whenever real trouble arose, the two soldiers always stopped fighting among themselves long enough to pound a few dozen Reds into submission. Thereafter, they went at each other's throats again, all for the sake of seeing who got the girl.[26]

The feminine presence during combat was a convention deplored by comic-book truth-tellers. One editor had rules against showing "beautiful women running around on a battlefield with their lipstick and silk stockings nicely in place," because, as he informed his readers, "it just ain't so!"[27] But in such books as *Tell It To The Marines, Fighting Leathernecks, Monty*

Hall of the U.S. Marines, and *Buddies in the U.S. Army* there were numbers of attractive ladies. Some of the war comics included "pinup" pages of girly art, suggesting something about the intended audience for the books.[28] There were also letters sections intended to link lonely servicemen with available female correspondents back home, a device that served equally well in war comics and romance comics during the early 1950s.[29]

The number of war-related comic books declined after the close of hostilities in Korea. Surviving titles placed emphasis not on Korea and the Reds but upon new stories about World War II, because the audience for war comics seemed to have a preference for explications of that earlier, tidier conflict.[30]

From the perspective of the mid-1950s, World War II was a safer place for comic books to be—and perhaps a safer place for their readers. World War II was more satisfying to contemplate than Korea, because it had been a declared war that ended in clear victory. In the popular mind, ambiguity had not characterized the American response to World War II. An evil enemy had been decisively defeated. None of that could be said about Korea, a police action having no convenient resolution. People were displeased with an episode that should not have happened, that could have been ended early with the Bomb, that lacked large numbers of highly visible heroes, real or imagined.[31] If they wanted a war in their entertainments, they could watch the Nazis get it in the neck again. If they wanted reliable heroes, they could rediscover the characters who had been waiting in the wings since World War II. These were heroes who had always been able to do everything anyway, and now it seemed that they could bash Reds, too—maybe as well as anybody, and certainly as well as our military forces. Maybe better.

From *Battlefield* 1:1 (Animirth Comics, Inc.: April 1952). Battlefield: TM & © 1952 Marvel Entertainment Group, Inc. All rights reserved.

THEY'LL START BUILDIN' THEIR HOLES RIGHT AFTER THEIR FIVE MINUTE BREAK, CAPTAIN, AN'...

SORRY, SERGEANT...NO FOXHOLE DETAIL FOR BAKER COMPANY! WE DREW THE SHORT STRAW... SO WE'RE MOVING UP...TO SPEARHEAD THE ASSAULT!

WE WERE ON THE GO AGAIN...BAKER COMPANY ONLY...SLOPPIN' THRU THE MUD! WE TOOK LAST DRAGS ON OUR BUTTS AN' THEN STRUNG OUT TOWARD OUR OBJECTIVE...THE RIDGE OF HILLS UP AHEAD...

THEN WE STARTED THE CLIMB! WE INCHED UP THE SLOPE ...HIDIN' BEHIND THE SLIGHTEST HILLOCK...THE SMALLEST FARMER'S FURROW...

THE SARGE WASN'T YAPPIN' NOW...AN' I WISHED HE WAS... 'CAUSE IT WAS TOO QUIET! I NEVER SAW THE ENEMY... BUT I FELT THEM! YEAH...FELT THEM SQUINTIN' ACROSS THEIR RIFLE SIGHTS AT ME! WAITIN' FOR ME TO GET CLOSER...

THEN, ALL OF A SUDDEN THE NIGHT LIT UP LIKE IT WAS DAY! THE GROUND SHOOK AN' THE CREST OF THAT HILL WAS AFLAME WITH RED MACHINE-GUN FIRE...

BR-RAK-KA-KA-BR-BRAK

3

64

5

The Cowboy Crusade

The heroic cowboy was a staple of American popular culture in the 1950s. He had been around in fiction since about the turn of the century, but he had never been the focus of as much media attention as he was in the post–World War II period, when his image seemed to be everywhere. In the early 1950s his ubiquity alarmed a number of observers, many of them academicians, who believed that because there was so much of him, there must be something to him; and, whatever it was, it probably indicated culture in a tailspin. In retrospect, his momentary elevation to the pinnacle of popular acclaim seems to have been largely accidental, the result of the brief coalescence of several media on the subject of a single persona. And in that regard, the heroic cowboy was a man for all seasons: the springtime of television, the summer of motion pictures, the autumn of radio, and the winter of pulp magazines. It was his heyday, and his exponents made the most of it.[1]

Comic books advanced his image as well, their publishers taking cues from the popularity of radio and motion picture cowboys, whether living or dead, because either way the ennobling process worked just as well. Silent film star Tom Mix, to mention a prominent case of posthumous fame, had been killed in an automobile wreck in 1940, but, as far as the children of America knew, he lived on through radio, helping to smash the Axis in World War II. By the time Fawcett Publications released the first issue of *Tom Mix Western*, its protagonist had been in the grave for almost eight years, and the audience could not have cared less. Because he was on the cover in an action photograph, because each issue was chock-full of stories about him, and because he was in advertisements between those stories peddling some sort of breakfast food and flogging decoder rings or some other significant item of cowboy paraphernalia, he was as good as alive, and—in view of what could now be done in his name, if not to it—maybe even better.

Tom Mix Western lasted five years (1948–1953) and 61 issues, which was a long time for a comic book, but not for a cowboy comic book. *Gene Autry Comics* ran for eighteen years (1941–1959) and 129 issues. *Roy Rogers Comics* endured for seventeen years (1944–1961) and 158 issues, probably some sort of cowboy record. Roy's faithful female companion, Dale Evans, starred in her own comic books between 1948 and 1959 but accounted for a paltry 46 issues. Still, she fared better than the horses, to judge by *Gene Autry's Champion* (19 issues, 1950–1955) and *Roy Rogers' Trigger* (17 issues, 1951–1955). In all, Roy, his wife, and his horse were responsible for 221 comic books between 1944 and 1961—not that Rogers needed any help. His own 158-issue total surpassed both *Red Ryder Comics* (152 issues, 1940–1957) and *Hopalong Cassidy* (135 issues, 1943–1959), which were, with Autry, his closest rivals. Other popular cowboys (such as Tex Ritter, 46 comic books, 1950–1959, and Rex Allen, 31 comic books, 1951–1959) paled by comparison.[2]

Whatever the heroic cowboy may have been on the big screen or the little one in the 1950s, in comic books he tended to function as detective, usually of the private variety but not infrequently under the aegis and with the badge of some local, state, or federal law-enforcement agency. He chased crooks, be they rustlers or despoilers of banks, railroads, stage-coaches, or other symbols of civilization, security, and economic development. He stood for law and order, peace and quiet, God and country, Mom and apple pie, just as he always had. And he was, according to the convention established as early as 1902 by novelist Owen Wister in *The Virginian*, a cowboy without any cows—but then the villains left him little or no time to pursue his career.

The heroic cowboy had long touted simple virtues in other media, and it was not surprising that he should do so in comic books. A comment about the sanctity of the home here, a wave of the flag there, and a nod of gratitude to the Creator in between, followed by a bit of the rough-and-tumble with those who needed it and a little gunplay with those who insisted upon it, and you had a wholesome, red-blooded American who neither smoked, chewed, drank, nor spat, was respectful in the presence of ladies, and revealed to men that he was a tough hombre to cross, on account of being so hard and smart and all.[3] He had less zip than a costumed superhero, of course; but he did own fancy clothes, fancy guns, and a fancy horse, and he was pleasing to the eye. He knew all about Nature from living in it, and he knew all about people from looking them in the eye, so he was a pretty fair role-model for anybody who needed one—and in the 1950s it seemed that there were many who did. Unlike the soldiers of Korea, the comic-book cowboy rode herd on no neuroses.

The 1950s were, as we have seen, troubled times, and the public had many concerns. But the era produced nothing to which the comic-book cowboy could not and would not speak. He was a good American who did what good Americans were supposed to do, and with a minimum of lollygagging. Juvenile delinquency might be the issue of the moment, so the comic-book manifestations of Gene Autry, Roy Rogers, *et al.*, would deal with disturbed or abused youth, runaways, or kids who simply had not been taught the difference between right and wrong. Toward the offending youngster, the heroic cowboy was firm but fair, making his points with sympathy and understanding but never wavering from the solid moral, ethical, and legal ground upon which he chose to plant his boots. The problem was that he could give a troubled kid no real stability because he had to ride away at the end of every story, but that was an essential device for any number of dramatic reasons, so nobody spoke of it. This sort of material tended to be saccharine anyway, and heroic cowboys were far better at pounding the stuffings out of full-grown criminals; but the point is that they addressed the issue and were among the most socially responsible of all comic-book types.[4]

Comic-book cowboys could address contemporary social problems because of the anachronistic nature of their existence. They went about on horseback and camped out at night and had to do with rather primitive Indians, but there was no historical context. They rode the mid-twentieth-century West, among cars and trucks and planes and speedboats and all manner of modern technological wonders, suggesting that the mainstream meandered freely through the outback and that western social issues were merely American social issues writ rural. Problems were the same everywhere; and the heroic cowboy could be expected to find them in his bailiwick with the same regularity with which an urban-dwelling super-hero might find them in his.

Drug use was a typical post-World War II concern. Drugs were responsible for crime and violence, and thus they constituted a worthy target for comic-book crusaders of various types, cowboys among them. After all, drugs could promote aboriginal aberration, as they did in the November 1950 issue of *Wild Bill Elliott Comics*, when drug use was blamed for an Apache crime wave.[5] In this instance, Elliott fell in with an agent of the F.B.I. craftily disguised as a cowboy, and together they cracked the case. They determined that "young braves" were getting "hopped up" on something at their dances, and it proved to be heroin, which the Indians were "sniffing" from porcupine quills provided by "their native magician." Quoth Elliott, "That would account for a lot of the crimes, robberies and worse." The heroic cowboy and the cowboy F.B.I. agent eventually rescued a girl from some "Apache hopheads" and busted the supplier, whereupon the agent and the girl walked off, arm in arm, leaving the heroic cowboy to his horse, as usual. Clearly, Elliott was inexperienced in the matter of ser-monizing in the wake of a satisfactory drug arrest, but in the

1950s one could always find a Rocky Lane to manage a line like "No one else will be contaminated by this evil stuff," while handcuffing a narcotics trafficker.[6]

In the comic-book West, nobody made the connection between drug addiction and crime as emphatically as Roy Rogers, who seemed forever mired in problems arising from both in the early 1950s. On one occasion, called in to investigate some rustling activities, Rogers learned that a local pharmacist, ostensibly treating the minor ailments of some tough characters, had begun injecting them with dope. Once he had managed to get them hooked, he raised the price of his drugs. "The rest was pretty much the story of all dope addicts, I reckon," Roy observed. "They sold what they had to raise money, and when that wasn't enough, they started stealing from other folks! In this case, what they stole and sold was cattle!"[7] Owing to Rogers's efforts, the F.B.I., an ever-present entity in the comic-book West of the 1950s, was able to crack the ring that had supplied the pharmacist with narcotics. Here was a suggestion that substance abuse on a small scale was never what it seemed. It was merely a minor aspect of something much larger.

When it came to polluting the western countryside with drugs and sapping its vigor as a preliminary step toward bringing the entire nation to its knees, nobody could top the Communists. And when it came to smashing Reds who were so inclined, nobody could top Roy Rogers working in conjunction with the F.B.I. In a 1952 story, Rogers intercepted a shipment of something-or-other intended for a spy named Carver. "It's dope," he exclaimed, upon opening the package. "*Heroin*— the stuff that's rotting the life and soul out of hundreds of thousands of addicts! The most fiendish weapon that the enemies of America have used!" He informed the spy that "a higher power than I will judge you . . . and a higher court than Judge Colt will take care of your sentence," and then he packed him off to the F.B.I., "before your bunch of subversives . . . can guess what has happened to you."[8]

Whether heroin was Communism's "most fiendish weapon" was problematical in *Roy Rogers Comics*, despite the assertions of the King of the Cowboys. Rogers had been able to bust Carver in the first place because of clues discovered in an earlier story involving Red efforts to poison the water supply of a new western defense plant with anthrax germs.[9] Saboteurs, it seemed, had reached an assistant engineer at the plant, gotten him drunk, and talked him into shutting down the plant's chlorinating equipment. Rogers went on to shut the spies down instead, to earn the gratitude of the ubiquitous F.B.I., and to express the hope that he could again work with federal agents. Six months later he did, breaking a case involving the spread of aftosa virus among western cattle ranches by a traveling medicine show peddling bottles of infected horse liniment.[10] Who in the world, the sheriff asked Rogers, would want to destroy America's beef supply with hoof-and-mouth disease? "Our country has enemies who would like to see that happen," Roy told the apparently naive lawman, "enemies who hate everything American!" Evidently so, if they had reached the point of waging biological warfare against us.

An enemy so inherently evil was clearly capable of anything, and the heroic cowboy who would do his part needed to remain constantly vigilant. Sometimes a fellow had to give up Christmas for the sake of the free world, as Rogers did when he helped the F.B.I. track down Red saboteurs in a snowstorm.[11] Usually, however, one encountered Communist plots and plotting Communists simply in the course of the day's activities. The discovery of a cave filled with weapons and money might signal more than mere criminal activity: It might be a cache left by Communists "to supply local rioters at a crucial time," as, "in case of hostile action by a future enemy, against big West Coast defense plants."[12] Or a runaway atomic scientist "frightened by his own discoveries" ("I *know* that if I were wounded and captured, and the enemy should pick my mind of certain secrets . . . millions of persons would die horribly!") might need to be rescued from Red spies chasing him across the western landscape. A fellow just never knew what to expect.[13]

Roy Rogers was not the only Commie-catching comic-book cowboy in the 1950s. Others included Buster Crabbe, who was known to pursue atomic spies operating in the West, and John Wayne, who traveled to the Middle East to catch Russians masquerading as Arabs ("Wait'll he wakes up—I think he'll answer to Ivan and pray to Moscow . . . ") to foment "nationalist" revolutions among "natives" colonialized by American oil companies.[14] But Rogers played the counterespionage game more often and to a greater extent than any of the others, as befit his status as America's foremost heroic cowboy.

That stories of Communist subversion beyond the Mississippi should figure so frequently in western comic books of the early 1950s proceeds logically from the socio-political context of the period. The spy comics featured activities of specialists often in the employ of supersecret government agencies. The war comics portrayed activities of highly skilled (if often psychologically shaken) fighting men, specially trained by the several branches of the military. Such publications might inform or indoctrinate readers, but their protagonists were largely isolated from normal society, even though they might operate from time to time within it. The average Joe might participate, but only by removing himself from his environment through some bureaucratic process, as enlistment in the military or application to some federal agency. The heroic cowboy served to fill in a large blank by demonstrating that a citizen might assist the government, out of uniform or without special authorization. True, the cowboy might on occasion be pressed into service as a deputy sheriff, but such assignments were temporary and would end with the story, leaving him free to ride away toward his next adventure. The cowboy, at bottom, was his own man; and however deep his commitment might be to doing the right thing, he nevertheless had some choice in the matter. He was not—could not be— ordered to do what he did. Rather, his actions followed from his senses of duty to country and responsibility to fellow Americans. Throughout, he remained largely a free agent.

The frequent involvement of the F.B.I. in the stories in *Roy Rogers Comics*[15] was certainly in keeping with the long-held policy of J. Edgar Hoover to advance a favorable image of the agency through popular entertainment.[16] The Rogers comics depicted an F.B.I. that was the first line of domestic defense against Communist activity. Its agents were the first you called in the event of trouble from the Reds, and they were the first to whom you responded whenever help was needed. It is of interest that Rogers was forever addressing Kenneth Brant, the F.B.I. man with whom he always worked, as "Mr. Brant" and never by any more familiar name, no matter what intimacy their mutual confrontations with the Red menace may have bred. Brant, in contrast, always addressed the cowboy as "Roy" or "Rogers," and the latter more often than the former. The "mister" business was no mere rangeland courtesy, inasmuch as Rogers was on a first-name basis with everyone who was not a villain, including the local lawmen who sometimes deputized him and were almost always his seniors by two or three decades. It was deference to federal authority, pure and simple; and it was uncharacteristic of the heroic cowboy operating in the egalitarian West, even in comic books. The odd notion that a society of freewheeling, irreverent cowboys could tolerate a "king" may not have seemed incongruous to an audience enamored of the Rogers persona, but in the comic books, Rogers's obsequiousness in the presence of Brant stood out like the proverbial sore thumb. It may have been an effective gambit, however, if the intention was to teach respect for the F.B.I. by having a primary role model exhibit so much of it.

Communists, by and large, faded into the western sunset after the Korean War, leaving the heroic cowboy to deal with villainy of a more ordinary stripe. Preachments of virtue rewarded still obtained, just as they always had, but they lost their political edge as cowboy comics drifted slowly through the becalmed years of Eisenhower's America.[17] Heroic cowboys were still out yonder, thataway someplace; and one could believe for at least awhile longer that if the nation—or the F.B.I.—needed them, they would ride back again and help us all breathe free.

6

Society and Change

The comic books of the post-World War II decade revealed an America in the shadow of the Bomb, beset by enemies with antithetical philosophies, and learning to deal with the several dissatisfactions of limited war in a barren place of questionable strategic value—all-new problems for an all-new world. In part, comic books functioned to maintain (if not to boost) morale in the face of a few unthinkable things, including atomic war and/or Communist takeover of the United States; and to that end, comic books told some truths and a great many lies. The truths concerned conditions (Korea, drugs, crime), and were depressing. The lies concerned the proffered resolution of problems, and could not entirely persuade or, in consequence, satisfy. Another part of the function of comic books was to indicate the norms against which aberrations like Communism might be measured. In that regard, comic books failed miserably.

Why was American society worth defending? Why was the American way of life better than anyone else's? What did our democracy really mean? What did we have to offer? Comic books simply could not manage successful answers to those questions, owing to the economic structure of popular culture. That which was mundane would not sell as entertainment, so comic books specialized in the atypical—costumed heroes, pistol-packing latter-day cowboys, talking animals—and their stock in trade had to be the normalization of the abnormal, as in the case of the Bomb. Comic books could get at "real life" only indirectly, because the norms they established were nothing more than the standards of aberration acceptable as entertainment. Normality is a statistical proposition, and "real life" could not contribute to the viability of comic books in the economic context of popular culture. Where the "real" impinged, as with Korea, exaggeration and caricature (as in the matter of the enemy) subordinated it for the sake of the market. Comic books took cues from reality, and then engaged in necessary acts of distortion. Thus, comic books tended to define America as much by what they did *not* present as by what they consistently offered to their audiences. If, for example, comic books could raise enough hell about Communism and its impact upon people in foreign countries, then America's stock would rise—not because anything substantive had been said about America, but simply because comic-book critiques situated America at the pole opposite something nasty. When comic books dealt with America directly, America sometimes became the nasty thing.

The postwar decade saw renewed interest in civil rights among black Americans, a logical result of World War II, in view of the fact that the same thing had happened after World War I. Harry S. Truman began to integrate the Army during the Korean conflict, and *Brown v. The Board of Education of Topeka* became the landmark civil rights case of 1954. And yet, to judge by comic-book representations of the period, there was no civil rights movement, nascent or otherwise, because there were hardly any black people in America, and the few in residence were perfectly content with bowing and scraping to the white folks who employed them as menials. They were stereotypes with rolling eyeballs, exaggerated speech, and the white-rimmed mouth reminiscent of minstrel-show performers; and their purpose was comic relief.[1] Otherwise, there seemed to be no blacks in comic-book America: no black heroes, super or otherwise; no black citizens living in

Gotham or Metropolis; no blacks out west; no blacks any-where in the United States.[2] There were, to be perfectly hon-est, a couple of black soldiers in Korea.[3]

There were blacks aplenty in Africa, and comic books had been frequent visitors to that continent since the late 1930s when they began to focus upon the adventures of Tarzan, re-printed from the successful newspaper comic strip. Tarzan was the lord of the jungle, as was Kaanga, introduced in *Jungle Comics* in 1940. Jo-Jo, of *Jo-Jo Comics* beginning in 1947, was merely the king of the Congo. Sheena was queen of the jungle in *Jumbo Comics*, beginning in 1938, whereas Rulah was a jungle goddess in *Zoot* as of 1947. Nyoka, only a jungle girl, began an eight-year run in 1945 (the comic book derived from a movie serial) and expired about the same time that Lorna became a jungle queen in 1953. And so forth and so on, if not in the abundant fashion of superheroes, perhaps, then at least in numbers sufficient to attract notice. Like Tarzan, the other jungle lords and ladies (and a few young heirs apparent) were white people who "ruled," or at the very least held con-siderable influence, over various "inferior" species, includ-ing lions, panthers, snakes, elephants, and black people. The status of blacks as items of fauna underscored the impe-rialist, colonialist, paternalistic, and racist thrust of the jungle comics—thrust otherwise indicated by specific descriptions of black behavior.[4]

Virtually every story chronicling the adventures of a white ruler of the jungle demonstrated several things about black Africans. They were incapable of self-rule, for instance. Left to their own devices, they inevitably got into trouble by selecting a rotten chief or falling for the fake pronouncements of some false god fobbed off on them by a devious shaman. Whenever such things happened, the Africans proved congenitally un-able to rectify the situation, coming to depend instead on the good offices of a bikini-clad white hero or heroine who was always bigger, smarter, stronger, and possessed of greater stamina and agility than any native and all wildlife. Africans in the jungle comics were superstitious, gullible, morally weak, and attempting to function with seriously diminished physical and intellectual capacities. Most of them could distinguish between right and wrong, but they succumbed regularly to the latter and were unable to effect the former without the intercession of a white hero. It was as if each jungle lord and lady presided over a vast nursery filled with dark children who were often disobedient and sometimes rebellious, but always lovable and, in the end, generally tractable—except for the few who had to be killed in order to save the rest. Without white executives to manage their affairs, the jungle folk would have slipped into chaos in a matter of minutes—or so argued the comic books.[5]

Many of the villains in jungle comics were white men, which hardly dispelled the racist overtones of the stories, inasmuch as black people were either their stooges or their victims. In neither case could much be said for black judgment. Blacks were depicted as too ignorant, too stupid, or too naive to see what was transpiring until their fat was frying in somebody else's fire—whereupon a white hero had to extinguish the flames.[6] In other comics the same thing held true of Indians, Mexicans, and the occasional Chinese. All required Caucasian intervention on their behalf. Natives were natives, it seemed, and wherever the white hero found them, they could be depended upon to have submitted already to liquor, drugs, Communism, scams of various kinds, and all sorts of criminal activity, either as perpetrators or as victims.[7] In other comic books, whites sometimes submitted to these things also, but nonwhites were especially susceptible. Moreover, whites tended to learn their lessons following rescue from calamity, whereas nonwhites were noticeably less educable and were unable to retain what instruction they did receive, owing to inherently short memories. As children, socio-culturally speaking, they could not help themselves. And in no case did their traditional cultures offer anything worthy of notice by white people.[8]

Comic books dealt with women in equally cavalier fashion in the postwar decade, but here the direction was sexist. The search for a strong female character could stop with Wonder Woman, although she was not without weaknesses. If she had fewer of them than any other female, it was because she had been invented by a psychologist to serve as a role model for little girls. The aforementioned jungle queens can be dismissed on several grounds, not the least of which involved their proximity to some kind of sidekick (usually a man but sometimes an animal) who bailed them out of trouble on a regular basis.[9]

Beyond carrying the banner for the white race, the jungle queens were there primarily for cheesecake, as were many other women. They catered to what passed for prurient interest among adolescent male readers, and sometimes they posed prettily for an older audience of servicemen. They reflected male criteria for the ideal woman: long hair, long legs, large breasts, physical agility, and proclivities rather more emotional than intellectual. Wonder Woman was a brainier babe, to be sure; but, except for having stumpier gams than most, she met the other criteria, role model or not. Even the females retained in comic books for their nuisance value—Superman's Lois Lane comes at once to mind—managed to look good most of the time.

Lois Lane, of course, demonstrated that it was perfectly all right for a professional woman to behave like a moron while mooning over the man of her dreams. It was expected that a handsome fellow could turn any female's brain to mush at first glance and without even trying. Indeed, he might do it by exhibiting complete indifference as much as by resorting to charm. Criteria for male conduct in comic books were established by artists, writers, and editors who were men—the same ones who established criteria for the appearance and behavior of comic-book women. So, in the matter of interpersonal and group relations, boys and girls received quite similar instructions from comic books, to the extent that they derived from the same set of male notions concerning the proper place of women in society.[10]

The messages to both genders on the subject of the relationship between the sexes were specific and consistent. Women were out to marry, or else they were not virtuous—and if that were the case, they were out to take advantage. Marriage was out of the question for heroic males because it cramped their styles, and so they managed to avoid it. Males could do as they pleased, and females were in for a good deal of frustration. The only places where women might achieve some degree of satisfaction were in the pages of romance comics, because they specialized in love stories from the female point of view. Romance comics focused almost exclusively upon the rituals of courtship, suggesting that the chase was everything, and proving it by losing interest in the protagonists once they had gone down the aisle. Here, too, women were offered up as emotional basket cases, responsible for their own misery because they either misjudged their men or tried too hard to play the field. Even though they might eventually find happiness, the implication was that they could have found it much sooner, if only they had not been so silly, devious, crass, or deceitful. Sometimes the women in romance comics were victimized by no-good, two-timing rats; but that was their fault too, just like everything else. It would never have happened if the ladies had possessed two grains of common sense.[11]

Only Little Lulu, in comic books since 1945, seemed consistently and assertively feminist in the postwar decade. She was a frumpy woman-child in a man's world ("No girls Allowed," said the sign on the boys' clubhouse); a Rosie the Riveter grown down; a pint-sized representation of the postwar female in constant rebellion against the low regard in which she was held, not only by most boys but also by some little girls whose behaviors suggested preparation for traditional female roles.[12] Little Lulu was tough and resilient, unlike most of her bigger sisters in the chauvinistic medium of comic books; and in consequence of those qualities—and the strength of her personality generally—she taught valuable lessons to the children (of both sexes) who followed her rather ordinary adventures. Little Lulu's contribution was a significant one, all things considered. What surprises is that, in the aftermath of a war in which American women played such a prominent part, Little Lulu was so dramatically alone in advancing the image of the competent and nevertheless thoroughly normal female.[13]

The appearance of Archie in the first comic book intended specifically for teenage readers (*Archie Comics*, Winter 1942–1943, following the boy's success as a minor feature in *Pop Comics*, beginning in December 1941) prompted the emergence of several teenage comic characters, all more or less patterned after radio's Henry Aldrich. Archie, his girl friends Betty and Veronica, his pal Jughead, and his rival Reggie represented an attempt to capitalize on a growing market; and soon, most of the major publishers had teenage characters to bolster sales. In the postwar decade, the comic-book teenagers reflected a rare industry effort at portraying supposed normality in situations that were at least marginally domestic. Kids had parents; the parents were usually baffled by the kids, who sometimes lost sight of parental authority; conflicts between parents and kids were brief and insignificant, happily resolved, and invariably humorous. Mom and Dad performed traditional roles: he brought home the bacon, and she cooked it. The kids were clean, well-dressed, mannerly (for the most part), and they attended school like they were supposed to do. The teenage comics offered idealized and light-hearted slices of postwar American life, keyed to the hopes and aspirations of the white middle class. They were sexist, racist, and ageist (in that older people were always dumber people), and thus were devoid of indications of the stresses operating within the modern world.[14] To the extent that *Archie Comics* and related titles were fairly long-lived, they testified to the popularity of that particular vision of unreality; but they did not match the appeal of another vision, namely the one contained in comic books belonging to the horror-suspense genre. These books offered an examination of America's dark side, specializing in grim views of society in general and of domesticity in particular.

Instructive are the eighteen issues of *Shock Suspenstories* published during the early to mid-1950s. Purposely or not, the comic book laid waste to the American family in a variety of ways, all of them suggesting its potential for destroying its membership, most of whom were demented anyway, to a greater or lesser extent. *Shock Suspenstories* presented tales of mousey wives who rose up at last and murdered tyrannical husbands, henpecked husbands who found the grit to murder shrewish wives, and abused children who engineered the deaths of worthless parents in order to go to live with reasonable aunts.[15] In one story, a baby—he was about three months old—murdered its mother and father because it resented being removed from the safety and security of the womb.[16] In another, a man decapitated a nurse (whose negligence had led to the death of his son), his business partner (whose corrupt practices had brought him to financial ruin), his maiden aunt (who had refused him the money to pay his business debts), his wife (who was having an affair with his best friend), and (naturally) his best friend—and then held a dinner party for the headless corpses, announcing his conclusion that people who did not use their noggins were clearly people who did not need them.[17] Interspersed were stories of kindly old ladies who roasted children in their ovens and erstwhile friends who abandoned folks caught in bear traps, causing them to have to gnaw through their own legs to escape.[18] *Shock Suspenstories* editor Albert B. Feldstein, an advocate of the O. Henry surprise ending, believed that comic-book yarns should have a certain twist to them, and many critics facetiously agreed that his were certainly twisted.

Such yarns as these conveyed the notion that the truly demented were plentiful in American society, and that, like Communists, they could be anybody. Here was a richly detailed and beautifully rendered literature catering to whatever paranoia the vulnerable reader might muster concerning the potential psychotic behavior of neighbors, friends, and kin. That lunatics could pop up in your kitchen like bread from a toaster was a commentary upon the inability of society to identify and isolate problems (or perhaps people) in advance of disastrous consequences; and by presenting the gory critiques, comic-book editors thumbed their noses at the several agents of social control, not the least of whom represented the forces of law and psychiatry. In some instances, the professionals were indicated to be even wackier (was it possible?) than the screwballs from whom they were supposed to be saving the average American.[19]

Among public servants, police were the most maligned in comic-book representations, regardless of editorial protestations to the contrary. Federal agents and deputized cowboys may have blunted the domestic Red Menace on a regular basis, but when ordinary cops tangled with ordinary criminals, somewhat different resolutions obtained. Crime was not supposed to pay, of course; and yet crime books had trouble with the theme, indicating all too often that it paid rather well. Even if the principal benefactors of criminal activity eventually died in a hail of police bullets, their end was a long time coming. And until it did, they managed to live higher on the hog than most of the American families whose offspring paid dimes to consider the wages of sin. On the one hand, comic-book criminals were exponents of a live-hard, die-young philosophy characteristic of the delinquent mentality that would find ultimate personification in the life (on screen and off) of Hollywood types like James Dean. On the other hand, and regardless of what the criminals did, it took the police an inordinately long time to catch up with them, no matter how well known their identities and their deeds. As a comic-book convention, the law's delay suggested the medium's preoccupation with the temporal splendors of criminal life rather than the spiritual rewards of being an awfully good cop. The focal point was the law breaker, not the blue-clad or plainclothes officer whose job was to bring him to justice.[20]

Comic books of the crime genre testified to the ineffectual nature of law by demonstrating the extent of the criminals' latitude. As well, they drew several distinctions between justice and "right," clearly indicating the difference between ethical absolutes and the disturbing relativity of human institutions. There was a certain ambiguity in the law (even in those seemingly simpler, pre-Miranda days) that could, if properly exploited by shady characters, result in the criminals' emergence unscathed from the system.[21] Here, real life impinged again upon the four-color world, to the disadvantage of convenient story-telling; and it was enough to make the home front as psychologically dismal as Korea. One convenience allowing the circumvention of law in a quagmire was the hero who was ostensibly a uniformed police officer, but who possessed a costume and a secret identity that allowed him to neutralize criminals by extralegal means, should circumstances block the normal avenues to justice—which, for the sake of the hero's adventures, was always the case.[22]

Comic books in the changing society of post-war America were, in the last analysis, male-initiated, male-oriented critiques of individuals and institutions that tended to reinforce such notions as black and female inferiority and to limn, purposely or not, a white, middle-class culture stressed nearly to the breaking point, beset by psychotics and criminals, and possessed of remedies that were only partially viable. Given comic-book statements of the American condition and the medium's enumeration of American problems, even the bright-clad heroes and their derring-do could not provide a hopeful prospect. Nor, given the post-war relationship between the medium and its real-world messages, could comic books offer much in the way of relief from dreary, depressing news. Children simply had no context for the comic books' curious and violent world—their youth denied them an overview—but some adults wondered if such fare were good for adolescent psyches. One or two decided that it was not, and they proceeded to bring the matter of comic-book content to the national forum. Popular reaction against the social commentaries of the once-innocuous comic book very nearly crippled the industry and removed the medium from the purview of its intended audience.

From *Thrilling Comics* 66 (Standard Comics, Inc.: June 1948).

86

88

89

90

94

7

Blaming Comic Books:
The Wertham Assault

The comic book, to the extent that it was "natural heir to the jaundiced eye of the purist in educational circles, the fundamentalist in the teaching of elementary English," came under attack by educators as early as 1940, when the medium was yet in its infancy. The more urgent concerns of the war years confined comic-book criticism to the academy, by and large; but in the late 1940s, given the nation's preoccupation with a variety of social problems, the time was ripe for fresh onslaughts by people who seemed to take comic books quite a bit more seriously than did the audiences for whom the entertainments were intended.[1]

The principal comic-book critic of the postwar years was Fredric Wertham, a New York psychiatrist who believed that prolonged exposure to the medium created disturbed, delinquent children. In 1954, after several brief preachments in the pages of popular magazines and scholarly journals alike, he published *Seduction of the Innocent*, the capstone of a seven-year study of the effects of comic books upon impressionable young minds—and a book whose title just about told it all.[2] Even if it did narrowly miss being a Book-of-the-Month Club selection, it was enormously popular, propelling Wertham into the national spotlight as a star witness at the hearings of the Senate Judiciary Subcommittee created a year earlier to investigate the causes of juvenile delinquency.[3]

Clearly, Wertham was a forerunner of the kind of media-oriented pop-psychiatrist later to be in vogue on television talk shows and syndicated self-help programs. The cynical view is that he recognized some of the problems affecting post-war America and simply chose comic books as the scapegoat for a couple of them. Then, having developed an issue, on which he, conveniently, was the only noted authority, he diligently rode it in the general direction of a healthy bank account.[4] Perhaps there was some truth in such a view; but it was also true that comic books had made themselves vulnerable to Wertham's attacks by taking considerable liberty in the matter of content. *Seduction of the Innocent* may indeed have been a blatantly opportunistic book. It was most assuredly a pompous, polemical, biased, and poorly documented one. But withal, it was squarely on target with regard to the excesses of comic-book publishers. Yes, corpses abounded in consequence of gratuitous, graphic violence; criminals were glorified; and criminal behaviors were explained to the point of justification. Yes, there was a heavy emphasis upon sex, and aberration therein was commonplace. And yes, there was enough to keep a psychiatrist busy for years, even if comic-book criticism had been his avocation instead of his career. Whether comic books caused juveniles to become delinquent, however, was entirely problematical.

Wertham tarred all comic books with the same broad brush. It was a necessary technique for a monocausationist who had chosen to assume that the medium was the message. Wertham could not afford to find redeeming qualities in any of the material under consideration, for to do so would have been to weaken the framework of his argument. Comic books, he asserted, stimulated children to commit violent, antisocial acts by providing detailed scenarios of those acts, accompanied by sets of ideas that were at best undesirable and at worst unhealthy. In either case, comic books were dangerous. His were data that, however superficial they might be, could not fail to alarm parents already concerned over everything else they had been reading in the popular press about delinquency, homosexuality, and related social problems.

Consider Wertham's evaluation of Superman, the character who had in effect created the comic-book industry in the late 1930s. Wertham stated that he had seen "troubled children, children in trouble and children crushed by society's punishments," and, by golly, just about every one of them had "Superman and Superboy comic books sticking out of their pockets."[5] As an exposition of cause and effect, that left something to be desired, but at least Superman escaped the more damning Freudian critiques Wertham leveled at other characters. The doctor's research confirmed the view (which he attributed to others) that stories about Batman and Robin were "psychologically homosexual," pervaded by "a subtle atmosphere of homoerotism." Indeed, the association of these two crime fighters was "like a wish dream of two homosexuals living together." And only "someone ignorant of the fundamentals of psychiatry and of the psychopathology of sex" would say it wasn't so—a splendid ploy for preempting the layperson's criticism of the critic.[6] As for Wonder Woman, she was the "Lesbian counterpart of Batman," a "frightening image" for boys and a "morbid ideal" for girls.[7] For a man of Wertham's background and training, the possibilities were very nearly endless.

Wertham simply ignored what he did not wish to acknowledge as worthwhile in the comic books under attack. He deplored racism and decried prejudice, for example, properly citing the host of jungle comics as prime offenders. But at the same time, he failed to note any of the several tales in comic books like *Shock Suspenstories* that deplored racism and decried prejudice. In one of that title's stories, a black man (the rarest of comic-book characters) was lynched by whites for, as it happened, a crime he did not commit. In another, a returning Korean War veteran discovered that the people in his hometown had refused to bury in their cemetery the buddy who had died saving the local boy's life—all because the buddy had been black. In a third story, a small-town, middle-American anti-Semite, having taken part in harassment that resulted in the deaths of two Jews, discovered that he had been born to Jewish parents who had been killed in an automobile accident, leaving him to be adopted by Christians. When the news got out, he was first shunned, then threatened, and finally beaten bloody by his former anti-Semitic cronies.[8]

Shock Suspenstories was but one of several comic books published under the aegis of Entertaining Comics (known in the business as EC), a group developed around 1950 by William M. Gaines from a line of largely unsuccessful comic books he had inherited from his father, Max Gaines, one of the pioneers of the medium.[9] Originally, the umbrella company had been Educational Comics, but when William Gaines added titles like *Weird Science, Crime Suspenstories, The Vault of Horror, The Haunt of Fear, Weird Fantasy*, and *The Crypt of Terror*, the line seemed to warrant a new name, although it still worked out to EC on the cover. There were other notable titles in the EC line, including *Frontline Combat* and *Two-Fisted Tales*, which we have cited in connection with the Korean War, and *Mad*, essentially a comic-book parody of other comic books. *Mad* did for the comics medium what one supposes the rest of the EC titles did for American society generally, which is to say that it delivered devastating critiques. All of the EC comics exhibited quality artwork and innovative editorial direction, and therefore they were as lightning rods to opponents of the medium. Their high visibility on newsstands made them natural targets in Wertham's campaign.

William Gaines and his editors at EC were of course aware of the mounting criticism of comic books. As if in response, they offered stories condemning individuals who acted as moral vigilantes out to preserve the public virtue. In some of these, the villains were hooded bigots belonging to organizations much like the Ku Klux Klan in philosophy and sartorial splendor. In others, the mob was less coherent and less well dressed. But all such stories contained references to Constitutional rights and the rule of law; and each suggested that the thoughtless actions of so-called moralists frequently backfired to everyone's disadvantage, including their own. Here, as elsewhere in EC's social criticism, there was much for Wertham and like-minded critics to ignore.[10]

The boldest—and surely the most unwise—of EC's anti-

Wertham counterattacks came late in 1954 in an "editorial" that ran in several of the EC books. It claimed that anyone advocating censorship of comic books (Wertham was then advocating a law that would forbid the sale or display of comic books to anyone under the age of fifteen) was quite possibly a "Red dupe." The editorial asserted that such Communist publications as *The Daily Worker* condemned comic books as instruments of Americanization and argued that the Reds were the group most eager to destroy the medium. It urged readers to challenge any critic of comic books—to "give him the *once-over"*—because, even if he were not a Communist, he was assuredly a dupe, having been influenced by the Party line. The editorial even managed to involve Wertham's name in a way that could lead indirectly to his identification with the dupes. William M. Gaines intended the whole thing as a grand joke, a response in kind to the tactics, no less than the bombast, of comic-book critics; but it happened that several United States Senators took the comments seriously, and Gaines found himself in the witness chair at the Senate Judiciary Subcommittee hearings on juvenile delinquency.[11]

By the end of 1954, the fate of many of the comic books of the postwar decade was already sealed. The controversy over possible relationships between comic books and juvenile delinquency had led the industry to move toward self-regulation, beginning in mid-1954. Publishers believed, with some justification, that they had better set their houses in order before the federal government stepped in to do it for them. They created something called the Comics Code Authority, an industry-based agency issuing guidelines that specified what was—and, more importantly, what was not—acceptable comic-book content. It provided publishers with a seal of approval, the appearance of which on the covers of new comic books was intended to reassure concerned parents about the wholesome nature of the fare inside. The Comics Code, as it was drafted and subsequently revised, simply prohibited most of what had appeared in comic books prior to 1954.[12]

Industry compliance with the provisions of the Comics Code ended what has since come to be known as the "golden age" of the comic book and, some have claimed, destroyed the creativity of the medium. The EC line, focal point of so much attention, succumbed quickly after 1954 to what its editors labeled finally as "hysteria."[13] No doubt they were correct, although again it is necessary to recall the extent to which they and their colleagues had aided Wertham's cause by providing him with so much ammunition. Gaines's *Mad* survived only by becoming a magazine. Many publishers simply folded their tents and left the comics field; but they might have had to do that soon anyway, given the growing popularity of television as the new adolescent pastime. Whatever the case, the number of comic-book titles appearing on newsstands dropped from approximately 650 in 1953–1954 to approximately 250 in 1956, as the publishers who remained in the business abandoned crime and horror comics and, more gradually, the myriad western titles.[14]

Juvenile delinquency did not disappear with the offending comic books. It merely ceased to be an issue holding public attention. Perhaps Americans simply grew tired of all those Senate hearings. Estes Kefauver took over the Senate Subcommittee in 1955 and tried to use its spotlight to obtain a presidential nomination, but the "hysteria" had subsided, as it always must, and he could not turn sensationalism to his advantage. Thereafter, the issue, like the Subcommittee, entered the bureaucratic limbo of unopened files and unread reports. The nation settled in for the cultural indolence of Eisenhower's second term.[15]

Surviving comic book publishers embraced anew the costumed superheroes, thinking them to be morally acceptable to an apprehensive public and, beyond that, economically viable. They were correct on both counts, although admittedly the concept of the superhero had to change for the sake of verisimilitude, whatever that quality might mean in the context of the post-Wertham medium. Certainly nobody anticipated a return to the escapism of the 1930s, and the superheroes comprised no signpost pointing back that away. Rather, they sought to be thoroughly modern, and they conformed to both the demographics of the marketplace and the psychology of the times.

In their post-1954 incarnations, the costumed superheroes were more neurotic than formerly—more human, the publishers claimed—for the sake of a new audience of college students from a television generation that had come to expect at least a modicum of realism in its entertainments. Perhaps because of this heady intellectual environment serving to house the once-lowly comic book, and also because of the promotional efforts of Stan Lee and the staff of Marvel Comics (creators of Spiderman, the Fantastic Four, et al.), there was journalistic talk in the 1960s and 1970s of a "new mythology" and of the comic book's elevation to the status of literature. There were fewer titles for smaller audiences, but publishers were more pretentious about their work, and each new offering appeared in company with a short ton of house-generated hype to indicate that it was some kind of instant classic.[16]

One should not forget, of course, the funny-animal titles, dominated by the creations of Walt Disney and characters from Warner Brothers' animated cartoons. They escaped criticism in the postwar period because they had always qualified as appropriate fare for children. Besides, parents and educators saw nothing sinister about rampant anthropomorphism, which could claim cultural legitimacy dating at least from the time of Aesop. Wertham himself pronounced them "harmless."[17] Still, the cynic might wonder what a determined psychiatrist could have made of a duck notorious for his immaturity and possessed of a set of seemingly parentless nephews in a bachelor household entered only occasionally by a sexpot of the species with whom aforesaid duck maintained an unfulfilled relationship. A curious condition (or perhaps not) in a society where fowl wore shirts but no pants. When one might easily recognize the racism of jungle comics, how could a critic fail to notice the predilections of this duck's billionaire uncle for ransacking underdeveloped countries in search of fresh treasure for his vaults? But here were animals, not people, and their intent was humorous, not serious. Under those circumstances, there was no cause for alarm.[18]

Whatever else may be said of the comic books published after 1954 (during the so-called "silver age" primarily associated with Stan Lee's Marvel books), it must be noted that they were less reflective of American society than their predecessors had been. The nation still had problems after 1954, but comic books would eschew analysis. They would not, for example, speak to Vietnam as they had to Korea. Indeed, they would scarcely mention it at all until long after its conclusion. Nor, until 1980 and all that the election of Ronald Reagan signified to Americans of whatever political stripe, would comic books carry much of the kind of social, political, or economic comment that had made them such effective mirrors of the post–World War II decade.[19]

Dr. Wertham wrought more than he knew and less than he hoped. He altered the content of comic books for thirty years, and he reduced substantially the number of comic books on the market. But he did not destroy the medium, nor could he garner sufficient support to win government regulation. The ultimate irony of his anticomic campaign may be that the specific comic books he cited to prove his arguments are today highly prized by collectors and carry premium prices on dealers' sale lists. Those pernicious items are still being read, whereas Wertham's critiques are now considered to be rather more curious than trenchant, and sit unopened upon the shelf.

In the broad view, Wertham must be seen as the central character in one phase of a cyclical phenomenon affecting popular culture. Comic books warranted attention after World War II for the same reason that every other relatively new medium has, before or since, especially should parents perceive it as a threat to inflame the imaginations of their children. As mothers and fathers in the last two decades of the nineteenth century sought to rid their homes of the detrimental influence of dime novels, so did parents of the late 1940s and early 1950s respond to warnings about the evils of comic books. By the 1960s the culprit was television, and in the 1970s and 1980s it was rock music on albums and tapes and videos. Nowadays, the suspicious thing is the videocassette player, allowing adolescents access to everything from the most ghastly of horror films to the most explicit pornography. Each reaction proceeds from a new technology or a new application thereof, and technology suggests change, as do social disorders.[20] Juxtapose the two, and it is simple enough to blame the technology for the disorder. As one of Wertham's critics observed in 1949, the good doctor's assault on comic books "illustrates a dangerous habit of projecting our social frustrations upon some specific trait of our culture, which becomes a sort of 'whipping boy' for our failure to control the whole gamut of social breakdown."[21] Americans have succumbed to that habit with some regularity heretofore, and they are likely to continue—especially with guidance from the next prophet of moral decline. But regardless of the cultural offering, any accompanying furor can only enhance its utility to the investigator looking for windows into the American mind.

FANTASTIC BRAIN DESTROYERS

From *Zip Jet* 1 : 1 (St. John Publishing Company: February 1953).

110

8

Terminus Ad Qvem

9 have referred throughout to the postwar decade, the period 1945–1954. And yet the chronology is unhandy. Our brackets (the end of the war and the end of a certain kind of comic books) defy convention. Customarily, one may discuss a thing "since 1945," suggesting that the text will bring us to the day before yesterday; or one may deal with "the Fifties," by which is usually meant Dwight Eisenhower's two-term presidency. Either approach will lead to a pause at 1952 to assess what followed: those were culturally sterile years, some historians think, though lately others have argued otherwise. As a child of "the Fifties," I find it all condescending in the extreme. In my family, Ike was a savior of sorts, presiding over the end to the foolishness that made Harry S. Truman try planting (figuratively, but with literal possibilities) my older brother in Korea. That aside, and at work in the liberal academy, I once tried to discover what was the matter with Eisenhower, the old soldier from Kansas whose critics said he spent too much time indulging himself in popular culture, notably paperback westerns. There was Nixon, of course, and John Foster Dulles's nuclear brinkmanship, and other unpleasantries like those. But, undeniably, Ike had more on the ball than most. Indeed, he was our last president to write his own English; and that means more to me with each new administration. But even *that* aside, how could he be linked with the nation's culture and roundly damned because some thought the culture did not come up to snuff? As a boy, I reveled in that culture, or at least the part with which I had anything to do: Saturday matinees, radio drama, television in its infancy (when I could watch it), bubble-gum trading cards, comic books, pulp magazines, and more.

Decades later, I acknowledged that a good bit of it had been sheer drivel; but I noticed also that what had replaced it represented no significant improvement. There were better technologies, better delivery systems for transmitting culture to kids, but content had deteriorated beyond belief. Except perhaps in the realm of popular music, the Sixties and Seventies seemed drab by comparison—and productive of considerably less cultural documentation to assist subsequent students of those periods. *De gustibus* and all of that, but for me the indicators of what we had become all dated from earlier times—from the Thirties, which linked culture with economy to help us cope; from the Forties, when politics resolved economic problems in some deadly ways and offered the misdirection of a "good" war; and from the Fifties, wherein we began learning to adjust to what we had wrought beneath Stagg Field and at Los Alamos, while examining ourselves, our society, and our enemies (who were, as Pogo wisely reminded, sometimes "us") with particular intensity. There were issues aplenty in those three decades. It seemed to me, first through nostalgic recollection and then in consequence of formal research, that comic books had touched them all. The trouble was, few historians had touched comic books, despite the corresponding (however coincidental) chronology of the medium.

The content of comic books from 1945 to 1954 mirrored the concerns, preoccupations, and beliefs of American society during the post–World War II decade. Occasionally, the mirror may have been concave, convex, or convex-concave, in the manner generally associated with reflections in the carnival fun house; but never was the distortion so great as to obscure the proper identification of the object at hand. As a mirror, the medium was sufficient and effective. It was not without flaws, but no mirror is.

Comic books from 1945 to 1954 reflected a society attempting to adjust to profound changes. America had won its war against the Axis in what its allies termed deplorable fashion, and Americans had been made to realize that they had more in common with their enemies than their national myths had led them to believe. Therefore, the postwar comic books took no delight in recounting the horrible fate of the Japanese at Hiroshima and Nagasaki, although they did rejoice in America's great technological achievement. When the Soviet Union developed its own nuclear weaponry, comic books followed the federal government's lead in declaring that such devices, even in enemy hands, threatened only America's enemies, and in demonstrating a strong belief in the survivability of atomic war.

Comic books pertaining to the Korean War were pessimistic exercises, reflecting the difficulty Americans had in working up enthusiasm for the sort of limited conflict that the Bomb had supposedly rendered obsolete. As well, the Korean War was not that at all, but an undeclared conflict, a protracted and deadly police action against minions (North Koreans) of stooges (Chinese) of Russians, who themselves had been America's allies not long before, in the war against Hitler. The comic books mirrored the political confusion of the day, the uncertainty of events, the concern over the pernicious nature of monolithic Communism. They suggested that spies and counterspies were more effective than soldiers in meeting and dealing with the Red Menace; and the notion made sense to the extent that the Korean War was news (and the pessimism was thus inescapable), whereas the doings of spies and counterspies were classified (permitting optimism as a function of literary license).

In times of stress, some sort of positive constant is always helpful to the national psyche; and if Communist insurgency, the Bomb, and Korea all pointed to the irrelevance of costumed superheroes, then more traditional types might be refurbished to respond more believably to new socio-political situations. Thus it was that Roy Rogers could become an anti-Communist cowboy in the early 1950s. Like those costumed superheroes, he was originally a product of the Depression, and he dressed almost as strangely as they did. But, perhaps because he was supposed to be a mere mortal with at least a modicum of contact with historical reality, he was better qualified than creations whose antecedents lay in somebody's recollection of Mount Olympus or the Old Testament to rally America toward resolution of a few geo-political problems.

Blacks and women were second-class citizens in comic books of the postwar decade—blacks, because they were either seldom seen or servile; women, because they depended so frequently upon the good offices of men. Blacks and women shared defects of intellectual capacity, according to comic books, or perhaps it was simply that they tended to be ruled by their emotions. Comic books revealed a world owned and operated by white men, wherein avenues to power were closed against all who were not white men. The unfortunates dispossessed by gender or ethnicity roamed, for the most part, the side streets and alleys and frequently the cul-de-sacs of that world. Within the structure of the story, they were generally props, those women and blacks (and Indians, Mexicans, and Chinese), supporting the scenery, or serving as handy victims, or providing comic relief. Again, comic books were mirrors, this time for a racist, sexist society which, at the time, took racism and sexism as part of the normal state of affairs.

It was an ageist society, too, although the word means more now than it did then. One might suppose that a medium for youngsters would advocate a degree of juvenile autonomy—or that it might even encourage a bit of playful anarchy. But comic books reinforced popular perceptions of traditional roles within the family: mother in the kitchen or cleaning the house; father at the office or other place of business; and both (but especially father) largely oblivious to their children, who nevertheless developed normally on account of school, peer interaction, or some innate desire for the approbation of adults in positions of authority. Even in comic books of the "teenage" genre, where the normal authority figures (parents, teachers, principals, police) were customarily buffoons, kids still managed to learn in school, obey the law, fulfill the expectations of parents, and otherwise demonstrate traits characteristic of good citizens. In ordinary family or school situations, children were creatures clearly superior to the adults with whom they had to deal; but they were also subordinate to them, in comic-book deference to the social system the medium served. In action-oriented comic books, heroes were the superior characters, and children—even those who were the heroes' sidekicks—had much to learn. Heroes, we note, were role models. Parents and teachers were not. Heroes were adults younger than parents and teachers and thus closer in age to their little companions, and to their audience. Indeed, the older the comic-book character, the more negative his or her image was likely to be. Whether villain or fool, the senior citizen was no object of veneration.

Comic books of the postwar decade reflected something of the moral equivocation associated with a society in crisis—or with a society that imagines itself in crisis. Normality is always a statistical proposition, and awareness of changes in numbers that pertain to something considered important will generally fuel commentary. Why the increase in the divorce rate? Did it foreshadow the end of the family as a basic national institution? Did that have anything to do with perceived growth of the homosexual population? Were we becoming a nation of sissies? How were these things related to the performance of American troops in Korea? Were juvenile delinquents (whose numbers were increasing) the products of broken homes? Did a broken home mean that Mom had too much influence on youngsters, or that Dad did not have enough? In view of the prevalence of such questions in the popular press, might one anticipate the imminent moral collapse of the United States? Comic books belonging to the horror/science-fiction genre regularly responded in the affirmative—but not so much, one gathers, from pessimism about the future of the nation as from a basic philosophical commitment to the proposition that human nature was sufficiently perverse to destroy the most stable of social institutions.

By 1954, of course, comic books were viewed by increasing numbers of critics not as mere symptoms of social malaise but as root causes of it—or at least of that portion affecting the nation's youth. Beset by all who sought convenient solutions to complex problems, the medium barely survived onslaughts by the civic minded. Comic books comprised a four-color scapegoat for ills that even their virtual extermination could not cure. Once the fact that no cure could be easily found became clear, the concerned public lost interest; but by then it was too late for the many publishers already driven from the field by single-minded critics. If nothing else, the mortality rate among comic-book publishing houses, circa 1954, indicated the undercapitalized status of the industry. Corporate giants were abundant in other branches of the entertainment business, but among comic-book publishers they were few and far between. So were the survivors of 1954.

That comic books were the sole components of the comic/cartoon spectrum selected for criticism in the early 1950s owed more to their manner of presentation than to their content. Racism and sexism were not uncommon in the animated cartoons of the day, for example; and animated cartoons were viewed by millions each week in the nation's movie theaters.[1] As well, lurid and unseemly material occasionally made its way into comic strips, staples of the daily newspaper and thus regular visitors in the American home.[2] Comic books enjoyed a smaller audience than either comic strips or animated cartoons, but theirs was a targeted audience—children, teenagers, young adults—and their presentations to it were made largely without restraint. Graphic violence brought most of the complaints; and here, in fact, was the one area in which comic-book producers took greater liberty than cartoon studios or comic-strip syndicates could dare to permit. Evisceration, disfigurement, torture—comic books showed it all, and a great deal more. The argument that some of them were textbooks for aberrant behaviors resulting in extensive tissue trauma may be casually dismissed nowadays, owing to the ubiquity of exploitative "splatter flics" (the various Halloween and Friday the 13th films) as the prevalent pastime of many youthful consumers of popular culture; but the fact remains that examination of certain pre-1954 comic books can be a stomach-turning experience. Such books, though relatively few in number in comparison to the hundreds of titles produced in the postwar decade, must persuade the skeptic that the concerns of some critics—especially parents and teachers—

were sincerely motivated by a desire to remove unpleasant impressions from the purview of the impressionable. Whether comic strips and animated cartoons were psychologically healthier amusements is perhaps problematical, but the strips dealt in a gentler way with human issues, and the cartoons were usually anthropomorphic and always absurd. Their content could not have initiated or sustained a broadly based critical assault.[3]

Would that we had some sort of viable, statistical measure of the effect of comic books upon juvenile readers—not to apply to Fredric Wertham's interpretation, but to evaluate the medium's influence in shaping subsequent attitudes and opinions. What views in adulthood may be attributed to childhood readings of comic books? We have more testimony about the impact of television proceeding from the postwar decade than we do about any other medium; and that is so, in my judgment, largely because of the pervasiveness of the medium and thus its perceived potential for causing harm to youngsters.[4] But, while one medium did indeed supplant the other, there is nothing empirical to indicate that television's images entirely replaced those of comic books or rendered their recollection any less potent.

When I was eleven years old, I acquired, at a school rummage sale, a coverless copy of what, years later, proved to be the fortieth and penultimate issue of *Two-Fisted Tales* (December 1954–January, 1955). Its opening story was entitled "Dien Bien Phu!" and concerned the failed French defense of that outpost in what was then known only as Indo-China. Told in the first person, the story ended with a panel showing the narrator's own blood spreading over discarded pin up pictures on the floor of the last French bunker, "even as the Red tide is spreading over Indo-China," for goodness' sake. It was a troubling story, and I read it many times.

I cannot say that the politics of "Dien Bien Phu!" disturbed me. By then, the "police action" in Korea had ended, my big brother was safe, and at school we were ducking and covering as per federal instructions—that is, we were diving beneath our wooden desks whenever a teacher flipped the light switch, persuading ourselves and the adults responsible for us that we could handle an atomic blast. Indeed, we would emerge from under our desks unscathed. This was in Chicago; and if we needed further evidence of our own security, we had only to ride the Illinois Central up to the Loop and observe the antiaircraft implacements and the Nike missile installations on the greensward along the Outer Drive. But there were no Commies overhead, and none in our neighborhood, that we knew of, anyway. And for most of us, the Red tide had ebbed—if, in our cowboy-and-Superman-soaked consciousnesses, it had ever really flowed in the first place.

Somehow, I never managed to forget "Dien Bien Phu!" Long after that ragged copy of *Two-Fisted Tales* and I had parted company, the story would rise to the surface of my memory, drawn there most often by current events. Indo-China became Vietnam, and Kennedy committed us to it, Johnson made a fetish of it, and those of us in college developed a keen interest in the Selective Service classification system. Occasionally, some journalist would reprise the French defeat at Dien Bien Phu, but for the most part it was overshadowed by outrageous political rhetoric, up to and including Lyndon Johnson's promise to "nail the coonskin to the wall" in celebration of an American victory. At such times, I remembered that old comic-book story. I could see the French officers drinking a final toast to flag and country and going out to die, and I could see the blood spreading across the bunker floor. I realized that repeated readings of "Dien Bien Phu!" a decade before had led me to conclude that the United States did not have a ghost of a chance to win a war—any war—in Vietnam.

Some thirty years after my first encounter with the fortieth issue of *Two-Fisted Tales*, I acquired another copy and reread "Dien Bien Phu!" This time around, it seemed to me that the story contained a warning, not about the futility of a land-war in Asia (after the advice of Douglas MacArthur), but about the importance of halting the spread of Communism. In fact, it was as much an early plea for American involvement in Indo-China as it was an antiwar tract. At age eleven, I had ignored that, noting only the massacre of French soldiers who, despite their formidable skill and training, were nevertheless outgunned by determined Commies in pith helmets. Not much of a nationalist in the mid-1950s (despite the best efforts of my teachers, I suppose), I did not assume automatically that American troops would succeed where elite French paratroopers had failed. Nor did I have any real idea why the people in the pith helmets fought with such vigor and determination. From the perusal of hundreds of Korean-era war comics, I was well aware of the shortcomings of the American soldier; but I could not account for the tenacity of the various Communist minions who were our enemies—at least not beyond the standard good-versus-evil dichotomy offered by popular culture in those days. At age eleven, though, I knew that it was difficult to be seriously and consistently bad, unless you happened also to be demented. And yet, comic books did not preach the existence of entire nations of demented people—or, as I discovered much later, they had not done it since the end of World War II.

During the Vietnam years, I often wondered how so many people could be so optimistic about the prospects for American victory. Not the politicians or the Joint Chiefs of Staff or veterans of earlier wars or right-wing clergy, all of whom had different axes to grind, but the people who were, or were to become, the soldiers who would do the fighting— how could they maintain the hope that a bit of trivia like "Dien Bien Phu!" had long since snatched from me? I have never met a veteran of Vietnam who recalled having read the story, or *Two-Fisted Tales*, or very many comic books of any kind, and yet we all belonged to a generation supposedly threatened by the sheer ubiquity of the comic-book medium and its messages.

Since American withdrawal from Vietnam, there have been millions of words written by former soldiers recounting their experiences during the conflict; and not a few of the memoirs proceeding from service in Vietnam have accepted the chore of explaining the preenlistment mentality of American troops. Almost without exception, the accounts stress the influence of motion pictures and television in establishing the norms of patriotic, masculine, American behavior. Middle-aged veterans now confess to early seduction by John Wayne,

Audie Murphy, and even Hopalong Cassidy. We must assume that the impact of screens, whether large or small, pushed other images aside, so that, even if these veterans ever contemplated comic books in the first place, the visuals wrought by New York and Hollywood were finally more pervasive and more easily recalled.

We have no similar body of memoirs from the people who opposed the war at home, especially in the late 1960s. If we did, perhaps we would learn who had been reading all those comic books that depicted war as something less than a blessed event. All we know with any degree of certainty is that millions read them—although we can say so only because we know that many millions of copies were printed and sold. Perhaps, as some have said, it was television, not Wertham, that caused the departure of comic books from the cultural marketplace. Perhaps the only children who read them in the early 1950s were, like me, those whose parents foreswore television until the middle of the decade or until they were prepared to accept the inevitability of the medium, whichever came last. But, that aside, there were so many comic books in the postwar decade, they must have meant something, and academics have taken a little too long in finding out what that is. Now that we have some idea of the lessons, perhaps it would be well to know who learned them.

Notes

Chapter 1

1. There were occasional exceptions; but, as Frederick Lewis Allen noted, perhaps books like John Steinbeck's *The Grapes of Wrath* (1939) would not have enjoyed so much popularity if they had appeared earlier in the decade, before people became accustomed to unemployment—or, as Allen said, complacent about it. For his assessment of popular fiction, see Allen, *Since Yesterday* (New York: Harper & Brothers, 1940), ch. 10. Good-natured acceptance of the various pronouncements of Will Rogers, who seemed to be able to get away with anything, perhaps stemmed from the fact that he appeared to be a harmless bumpkin.

2. Andrew Bergman, *We're in the Money: Depression America and Its Films* (New York: New York University Press, 1971); David Zinman, *Saturday Afternoon at the Bijou* (New Rochelle, N.Y.: Arlington House, 1973).

3. William H. Young, Jr., "The Serious Funnies: Adventure Comics During the Depression, 1929–38," *Journal of Popular Culture* 3:3 (Winter 1969): 404–27. See also Ron Goulart, *The Adventurous Decade* (New Rochelle, N.Y.: Arlington House, 1975). The Depression changed the newspaper comics in other ways, as well. Chic Young's Blondie, originally in 1930 a gold digger in pursuit of Dagwood Bumstead, a millionaire's son, became an ordinary housewife in 1933 when she married the disinherited heir who thenceforth had to work for a living. Five years later, Ernie Bushmiller shifted the focus of "Fritzi Ritz" from the Hollywood starlet, whose name the strip bore, to her niece, Nancy, a child who associated with a ragamuffin named Sluggo. In contrast, George McManus's monied characters, Jiggs and wife Maggie, maintained the economic status they achieved during the 1920s, but retained reader acceptance during the 1930s by flashing back with some regularity to their early days as virtually penniless Irish immigrants. Otherwise,

the public seemed in no mood to contemplate the doings of the elite. See Dean Young and Rick Marschall, *Blondie and Dagwood's America* (New York: Harper & Row, 1981); Brian Walker, *The Best of Ernie Bushmiller's Nancy* (New York: Henry Holt and Company, 1988); and George McManus, *Jiggs Is Back* (Berkeley, Calif.: Celtic Book Company, 1986).

4. As had "big little books," a generic term for chubby novelizations of comic strips, rendered for children with facing-page artwork for each page of text, and "feature books," a generic for large-format reprints of newspaper strips. Both were forerunners of the modern comic book.

5. Ron Goulart, *Ron Goulart's Great History of Comic Books* (Chicago: Contemporary Books, 1986), and James Steranko, *The Steranko History of Comics*, 2 vols. (Wyomissing, Pa.: Supergraphics, 1970–1972), as well as other volumes discussed in the Bibliographical Note below, provide ample information on the early history of the medium, the emergence of heroes, and other related matters. A splendid collection of comic-book material from ca. 1937 to 1950 is *The Greatest Golden Age Stories Ever Told* (New York: DC Comics, Inc., 1990).

6. The first issue of *Superman*, appearing during the summer of 1939 and elaborating upon the hero's origin, reiterated that Superman had arrived as a baby, via spaceship, and was adopted by Mr. and Mrs. Kent. It indicated that the "love and guidance of his kindly foster-parents was to become an important factor in the shaping of the boy's future." When he was grown and they were dead, he "decided he must turn his titanic strength into channels that would benefit mankind. And so was created—Superman, champion of the oppressed, the physical marvel who had sworn to devote his existence to helping those in need!" A reprint of the story is contained in *Superman from the Thirties to the Seventies* (New York: Crown Publishers, 1971). If that were not sufficient indication of wholesomeness, consider the remarks of Mort Weisinger, an editor for National Periodical Publications (originally Detective Comics, or just plain DC), the publisher of the assorted titles in which Superman appeared: "Moses was a baby and they put him in a boat and sent him down the river and he was adopted by *new* parents. Superman was a baby and his parents put him in a *spaceship* and sent him to be saved—to Earth. There's your whole analogy." Dennis O'Neil, ed., *Secret Origins of the Super DC Heroes* (New York: Warner Books, 1976), 15. Jerry Siegel and Joe Shuster, *Superman Archives 1* (New York: DC Archive Editions, 1989), reprints the first four issues of *Superman*, 1939–1940.

7. Gary H. Grossman, *Superman: Serial to Cereal* (New York: Popular Library, 1977); Dennis Dooley and Gary Engle, eds., *Superman at Fifty: The Persistence of a Legend* (Cleveland: Octavia, 1987).

8. All this stems from a reaction to various notions in John L. Fell, *Film and the Narrative Tradition* (Norman: University of Oklahoma Press, 1974), and Alice G. Marquis, *Hopes and Ashes: The Birth of Modern Times, 1929–1939* (New York: The Free Press, 1986). Fell touches briefly on comic books, and Marquis says nothing about them.

9. Uncle Sam battled the "Purple Shirts," a gang of Nazi-like villains

bent on fomenting revolution among migrant "Oakies" [*sic*] in *National Comics* 1 (Quality Comics Groups: July 1940); Captain America was revealed punching Hitler in the mouth on the cover of *Captain America Comics* 1 (Timely: March 1941); *Big Shot Comics* 13 (Columbia Comic Corporation: May 1941) featured Skyman ("America's National Hero"), Captain Devildog of the U.S. Marines, and Spy-Chief (an F.B.I. agent named Jeff Cardiff) all battling fifth-columnists and other "foreign" threats to America and to its overseas interests; and the Fighting Yank foiled a Nazi plot to establish a dictatorship in America in *Startling Comics* 10 (Better Publications: September 1941). Here and hereafter, publication information is taken from indicia, not from the varying data contained on the front covers of comic books.

10. Europeans understood all this a good deal earlier than Americans did, because Europeans were in the soup first. H. G. Wells, explaining in a preface to his *Seven Famous Novels* (New York: Alfred A. Knopf, 1934), x, why he no longer wrote "imaginative books," observed: "The world in the presence of cataclysmal realities had no need for fresh cataclysmal fantasies. That game is over. Who wants the invented humours of Mr. Parham [a Wells character in a "sarcastic fantasy" about dictators] in Whitehall, when day by day we can watch Mr. Hitler in Germany? What human invention can pit itself against the fantastic fun of the Fates?"

11. Comic books support the various contentions of John W. Dower, *War Without Mercy: Race and Power in the Pacific War* (New York: Pantheon Books, 1986), even though Dower chose to ignore them. Of the foregoing, *Cat-Man Comics* 20 (Et-Es-Go Magazines: October 1943) is a prime example, inasmuch as Cat-Man strangled Hitler on the cover but pursued Japanese saboteurs inside. Virtually any hero-oriented comic-book issued during the war years will indicate enemy stereotypes, but see the covers of *Startling Comics* 22 (Better Publications: July 1943) for German monocles, and *Startling Comics* 23 (Better Publications: September 1943) for Japanese teeth. Among the most graphic, bizarre, outré, and ultimately disgusting stereotypes of Axis villains were to be found in *Air Fighters Comics* (Hillman Periodicals), beginning with the second issue in November 1942. The rather surprising cover of *The United States Marines* 3 (Magazine Enterprises, 1944) revealed a bespectacled, toothy Japanese with the body of an octopus being burned to a crisp by a leatherneck with a flamethrower. Captain Midnight, whose "blazing uniform . . . spells terror to Axis rats," from time to time faced one named Von Togo, an Oriental who spoke with a thick German accent. See "Terror in Tibet," *Captain Midnight* 18 (Fawcett Publications: March 1944). See also "Comic Strips at War," *Look* (November 30, 1943): 51–53. *How Boys and Girls Can Help Win the War* (The Parents' Institute: 1942) was a self-help comic book that lectured children on everything from eating right and keeping fit to buying bonds and collecting scrap to learning first aid and preparing for air raids.

12. Don Thompson, "Ok, Axis, Here We Come!," in Dick Lupoff and Don Thompson, eds., *All in Color for a Dime* (New York: Ace Books, 1970), 121–42.

13. Superman's absence from the European and Pacific theatres was explained in the McClure Syndicate's newspaper comic strip, February 15–19, 1943, a more sophisticated rendition of the character, intended for adult audiences. Clark Kent failed his physical because of Superman's X-ray vision. Inadvertently, he peered through a wall and read a different eye chart in the next room, thus proving himself to be blind as a bat. The strip for February 17 contained both Kent's assertion that the "United States Army, Navy and Marines are capable of smashing their foes without the aid of a *Superman*" and his promise to fight "right here at home, battling the saboteurs and fifth columnists."

14. "Captain Marvel and the War of the Trolls," *Whiz Comics* 32 (Fawcett Publications: July 10, 1942). Adolf-Puss and Blabbermouth Musso were leaders of the Nasties, no less. C. C. Beck, the artist responsible for many of the vintage Captain Marvel adventures, deplored this sort of thing, believing that the war effort was detrimental to the talents of comic-book creators because "all the heroes had to be out there stopping bullets and tweaking Hitler's nose and punching Hirohito in the teeth and everything else. We had to do that. We were ordered. We had to do it for propaganda purposes." See "'With One Magic Word . . . ' An Interview with C. C. Beck," *The Comics Journal* 95 (February 1985): 60. All the heroes were on our side, and so, the religionists proclaimed, was God; but how comforting it was to know that Santa Claus, trading sleigh for airplane, was our foremost bombardier, hurling brickbats and explosives at Japanese and Germans, as in Sid Lazarus's "Twas the Night Before Christmas," *The Blue Beetle* 28 (Holyoke Publishing Company: December 1943).

15. Artist Howard Nostrand, explaining the financial success of comic-book publishers during World War II, recalled that "guys in Army camps were starved for *anything* to read. You could sell anything you printed," if government restrictions on paper could somehow be circumvented. According to Nostrand, that fact accounted for the publication of a great deal of garbage. "Nostrand By Nostrand," *The Comics Journal* 95 (February 1985): 80.

16. This sort of thing has come to be known as "good girl art," and although its antecedents may be found in the pulp magazines of the 1930s, it flowered in comic books of the World War II era. Books containing scenes of female bondage and what specialists term "headlight" covers (i.e., comic-book covers featuring protruding breasts) are nowadays highly prized among collectors. See Carl Macek, "Good Girl Art—An Introduction: Why It Was and What It Is," in Robert M. Overstreet, *The Comic Book Price Guide, 1976–77* (Cleveland, Tenn.: By the author, 1976), 38–43. Virtually all of the *Fight Comics* and *Rangers Comics* published under the Fiction House umbrella during World War II carried covers exhibiting the headlight-bondage syndrome. According to Trina Robbins and Catherine Yronwode, *Women and the Comics* (N.p.: Eclipse Books, 1985), 52, Fiction House employed around two dozen women as artists, writers, and editors during World War II. Several Fiction House titles were produced by the studio of S.M. (Jerry) Iger;

and, beginning in 1940, scripts reflected the influence of Ruth Roche, Iger's eventual business partner. So, women were not entirely without responsibility for the "good-girl art" imagery of the postwar decade. See Jay Edward Disbrow, *The Iger Comics Kingdom* (El Cajon, Calif.: Blackthorne Publishing, Inc., 1985).

17. Consider *Captain Flight Comics* 10 (Four-Star Publications: December 1945), the penultimate issue in the series. The cover depicted a costumed hero (whose headgear resembled some sort of fish) leaping from a jet plane (which was painted to resemble some sort of snake) into the open cockpit of a prop-driven plane to strangle the pilot and (presumably) rescue the shapely young thing who was tied to the wing—and all of this took place above the clouds. Whoever that masked man was, he was not to be found inside the book. He was not Captain Flight or Red Rocket or Deep Sea Dawson or Ace Reynolds or Secret Agent 2 B-3 or anybody else. Stories concerned Captain Flight's pursuit of Japanese "sky pirates," Secret Agent 2 B-3's successful effort to save the Suez Canal from Nazis, Red Rocket's involvement with a peace conference in 2042 which was attended by the trouble-making Nazanians, and so forth. The final story concerned Captain Dash, an aviator who looked suspiciously like aforesaid Captain Flight—and who proved to be Captain Flight on the last page, because editors forgot to alter the text in what was obviously a backlog story. Indeed, most of the issue was backlog, including the cover.

Chapter 2

1. Paul Boyer, *By the Bomb's Early Light: American Thought and Culture at the Dawn of the Atomic Age* (New York: Pantheon Books, 1985); Ferenc Morton Szasz, *The Day the Sun Rose Twice: The Story of the Trinity Site Nuclear Explosion, July 16, 1945* (Albuquerque: University of New Mexico Press, 1984), ch. 8.

2. Spencer R. Weart, *Nuclear Fear: A History of Images* (Cambridge: Harvard University Press, 1988), provides useful background on the pre-Bomb development of these notions, noting especially the preoccupation of some World War II-era comic-book heroes with radioactive rays, e.g., Superman with Kryptonite. Rays were dangerous and could easily be used by villians, but heroes like Superman, Batman, and Captain Marvel could always overcome—the villains, if not the rays. See also Boyer, *By the Bomb's Early Light*, 25–26, and Charles Wolfe, "Nuclear Country: The Atomic Bomb in Country Music," *Journal of Country Music* 6 : 4 (January 1978): 4–22, and consider the music in *Atomic Cafe: Radioactive Rock 'n Roll, Blues, Country & Gospel* (Rounder Records 1034), coproduced and with notes by Wolfe.

3. Of this, John Hersey, *Hiroshima* (New York: Alfred A. Knopf, 1946), was the principal indication. It first appeared in *The New Yorker*, was a Book-of-the-Month Club selection in 1946, and had entered paperback publication by 1948.

4. The naïve optimism of the day has been captured nicely in the docu-

mentary film, *The Atomic Cafe* (1982). See also JoAnne Brown, "'*A* Is for *Atom, B* Is for *Bomb*': Civil Defense in American Public Education, 1948–1963," *The Journal of American History* 75: 1 (June 1988), 68–90.

5. See, for example, *Li'l Pan* 7 (Fox Features Syndicate: February–March 1947).

6. See the inside front cover of *Ken Maynard Western* 6 (Fawcett Publications: October 1951).

7. "Assault on Target UR-238," *Atom-Age Combat* 3 (St. John Publishing Company: November 1952).

8. Compare "Atomic Attack," *Atomic Attack* 6 (Youthful Magazines: March 1953), wherein repeated atomic blasts had little or no effect upon either U.N. forces or the Reds, in another futuristic yarn. "The Atomic Witch Doctor," *Police Comics* 109 (Comic Magazines: November 1951), demonstrated that atomic fallout was not harmful to Americans, Reds, or natives living near Bikini.

9. *Atomic War!* 1 (Junior Books: November 1952).

10. "The Monarch of the Sargasso Sea," *Wonder Woman* 44 (National Periodical Publications: November–December 1950).

11. "Captain Marvel Battles the Bug Bombs," *Whiz Comics* 150 (Fawcett Publications: October 1952).

12. The Bomb was comic-book evidence that the United States had achieved a high level of civilization. See "The Statue of Liberty Play," *Super-Magician Comics* 5:5 (Street & Smith: September 1946).

13. The first Godzilla movie came to America in 1956. It was reedited from a 1954 Japanese film, *Gojira*.

14. See James Gilbert, *Another Chance: Postwar America, 1945–1968* (Philadelphia: Temple University Press, 1981), ch. 3, for a summary.

15. For two such small lessons, see "Marvel Boy and the Lost World" and "Panic!" in *Marvel Boy* 1 (Marvel Comics: December 1950).

16. Even "Atom Bomb!," *Two-Fisted Tales* 33 (Fables Publishing Company: May–June 1953), a powerful supposition about the effects of the Nagasaki blast on one Japanese family, could not escape an upbeat coda. The story ended with statistics—29,793 people killed, 18,409 homes destroyed—but promised that "*hope* was not destroyed in Nagasaki! And life nurtured by hope, blooms again!" And not only that, there was "*hope* in the whole world!" All this appeared above a final drawing of a smiling Japanese child running off to school, books beneath his arm, pursued by a playful puppy. In the background, factory chimneys belched smoke, and workers set about rebuilding the city. Even in stories from the horror or science-fiction genres, usually *something* survived atomic holocaust. In "The Arrival," *Shock Suspenstories* 8 (Tiny Tot Comics: April–May 1953), for example, rats inherited the earth and became a great race.

Chapter 3

1. It was asked in "Underground Empire," *Headline Comics* 10 (American Boys' Comics: Mid-Winter 1944), a story that spoke of Hitler's supposed

prior death in Europe. If this was not based on the July 1944 assassination attempt, it suggests a postdated issue. Whatever the case, the story line indicated that the war in Europe was all but over, so Hitler moved to Yellowstone. In *Target Comics* 7 : 3 (Premium Service Company: May 1946), Japanese saboteurs were attempting to ignite our national forests. In "Mein Kampf—Post-War Version," *Master Comics* 68 (Fawcett Publications: May 1946), Radar, the "international policeman," foiled a megalomaniacal German house painter named Fritz Kraut, who based his attempt to gain dictatorial power on the assumption that Hitler had been "too soft-hearted." Over a year later, Radar was still on the heels of "underground Nazi organizations" in "Food Train Menace," *Master Comics* 84 (Fawcett Publications: October 1947). In *Sparky Watts* 5 (Publication Enterprises: 1947), a costumed hero named Skyman fought against resurgent Nazis in the Amazon jungle. And so forth.

2. The political considerations of the period are discussed in Eric F. Goldman, *The Crucial Decade: America, 1945–1955* (New York: Alfred A. Knopf, 1956). A useful context is afforded by Michael Vlahos, "The End of America's Postwar Ethos," *Foreign Affairs* (Summer 1988): 1091–1107.

3. Frederick Lewis Allen, *The Big Change: America Transforms Itself, 1900–1950* (New York: Harper & Row, 1952), 278–83.

4. John D. Deene has identified *The Thing from Another World* as a "bipartite monster movie" in "Society and the Monster," reprinted in Roy Huss and T. J. Ross, eds., *Focus on the Horror Film* (Englewood Cliffs, N.J.: Prentice-Hall, 1972), 127–29. Such a film "reflects the concern of society with the struggle for power within the bipolar world" of 1945–1955. In some quarters, comic-book publishers were as reluctant to identify Russia as the evil empire as Hollywood was to burst the bubble of science-fiction allegory by naming names. Thus, in "Insurrecto Island!," *Boy Commandos* 16 (World's Best Comics Company: July–August 1946), the anonymous enemy was a revolutionary nation attempting to overthrow an honest republic, while in the final story in *Dick Cole* 1 : 3 (Premium Group of Comics: April–May 1949), the spies trying to steal a military academy biochemist's secrets of food production were "agents of a foreign power." Blackhawk, who emerged from World War II as the leader of an independent squadron of international fighter pilots, was frequently involved with combatting the expansion of an unnamed nefarious government during the postwar decade, as in "The Rajah of Ramastan" and "The Casbah," *Blackhawk* 37 (Comic Magazines: February 1951), and "The Root of Evil," *Blackhawk* 51 (Comic Magazines: April 1952). Reference was usually to "an aggressor nation" or "a dictator nation," but occasionally, as in "Whip of Montelon," *Blackhawk* 51, there was specific mention of "Reds." Blackhawk and his men were international policemen dedicated to the cause of world peace.

5. Even if they were not always bigger, our guys were tougher and smarter, as demonstrated in *Little Al of the F.B.I.* 10 (Ziff-Davis: 1950), despite its number, the first of the series. Little Al broke up Communist cells in the United States. *Little Al of the Secret Service* 10 (Ziff-Davis: July–August

1951), also a first issue, suggested something about the interchangeability of bureaucratic parts. Even smaller than Little Al was Dan Tayler, a child offered up as a detective. See "The Spy Menace!," *Boy Detective* 3 (Avon Periodicals: February 1952). And, of course, teenagers could do their part, too, as in "My Brother Is a Spy," *Young Men* 5 (Interstate Publishing Corporation: November 1950).

6. Treasury Agent Pete Trask was among the most hard-boiled of the federal Commie hunters in comic books, at least in the matter of snappy dialogue. Snookered once by "the most beautiful Chinese gal" he ever met—and a Red Chinese agent to boot—Trask remarked to a colleague: "I'm a chivalrous character, Charley, but I think I could choke that gal and laugh fiendishly while I did it." See "The Girl with Death in Her Hands," *T-Man* 2 (Comic Magazines: November 1951). In "Pipeline to Peril," *T-Man* 9 (Comic Magazines: January 1953), Trask told a Red agent, "I want to ruin your face a little." Slugging the Russian, Trask said, "That's for everything your rotten soul ever thought about!"

7. For the deaths of a few thousand Russians, see "Dirigible of Doom," *Spy Fighters* 5 (Classic Syndicate: November 1951).

8. See, for example, "Blitzkrieg Boomerang!," *War Victory Adventures* 2 (Family Comics, Inc.: August 1943), concerning the Battle of Stalingrad; "Manshuka, the Girl Who Fought a Regiment," *Real Life Comics* 20 (Nedor Publishing Company: November 1944); or consider the involvement of Ivan Igoroff with an American, an Englishman, and a Chinese in the "cause of world brotherhood" in "The Four Musketeers," *Air Ace* 2 : 3 (Street & Smith: May 1944). Russians were prominent allies in the Ball Syndicate's newspaper strip, "Stony Craig of the Marines," beginning in the late 1930s. The comic-book manifestation, with that enormous Russian, Sergei the Valiant, prominent on the cover, was *Stony Craig* (Pentagon Publishing Company: 1946). These and other comic-book items were ephemeral and did not return to haunt their creators in the manner of some Hollywood films, such as *The North Star*, *Song of Russia*, and *Mission to Moscow* (all 1943). In the early 1950s, *The North Star* was reedited to alter its pro-Soviet, anti-Nazi message. It was cut from 105 minutes to 82 minutes and retitled *Armored Attack* to go along with its new anti-Soviet, anti-Nazi message.

9. "The Great Betrayal," *Battle* 20 (Foto Parade: May 1953).

10. "Formosa!," *War Comics* 21 (U.S.A. Comic Magazine Corporation: September 1953).

11. "He Died for the Cause!," *Combat* 11 (Atlas News Company: April 1953) was an entirely typical preachment on the subject of fanatical Communism. ("To a Communist, his cause is everything! Human emotions . . . love, loyalty, friendship mean nothing!") The willingness of the oppressed to revolt with American encouragement was pursued in "Trial by Terror," *T-Man* 9, and "Mind Assassins" and "Red Minder Incorporated," *T-Man* 13 (Comic Magazines: November 1953).

12. "Terror in Tibet," *Kent Blake of the Secret Service* 3 (20th Century Comic Corporation: September 1951).

13. "Appointment in Albania," *Spy Fighters* 5 (Classic Syndicate: November 1951).

14. "Trail of Doom," *Spy Cases* 10 (Hercules Publishing Corporation: April 1952).

15. And no matter who else was supposed to be in charge. "The British had to call in American spy-fighters to wipe out the . . . 'Menace in Malaya,'" according to *Spy Cases* 8 (Hercules Publishing Corporation: December 1951).

16. Consider the garbled messages and mixed metaphors of "The Marvel Family Battles the Democracy Smasher," *The Marvel Family* 67 (Fawcett Publications: January 1952), and "Corpses . . . Coast to Coast," *Voodoo* 14 (Ajax/Farrell: March–April 1954), which attempted to say something about the Red Menace, democracy, atomic bombs, and all of that, with pathetic results. Even early on, when some comic books flirted with the notion of having American atomic scientists sell out to the highest bidder (presumably the Russians), as in "Ace of the Newsreels," *Crown Comics* 5 (Golfing, Inc.: 1945), the prospect did not please and the plot was not often repeated. But see "The Television Spies," *All Top Comics* 10 (Fox Feature Syndicate: March 1948). In the pre-Rosenberg years, such things defied belief.

17. The banner headline for *Spy Cases* changed from "Danger! Spies at Work! Real Spy Cases!" on the eighth issue to "Spies at War! Battlefield Adventures of Actual Spies" on the tenth issue. *Spy Fighters* 9 (Classic Syndicate: July 1952) had Clark Mason continuing to function as a federal agent, albeit in an Army uniform. Inasmuch as these people always operated in company with ordinary frontline grunts, one might wonder upon whom they were supposed to be spying.

Chapter 4

1. Dr. Benjamin Spock, *The Common Sense Book of Baby and Child Care* (New York: Duell, Sloan and Pearce, 1946); Alfred C. Kinsey, Wardell B. Pomeroy, and Clyde E. Martin, *Sexual Behavior in the Human Male* (Philadelphia: W. B. Saunders Company, 1948); Philip Wylie, *Generation of Vipers* (New York: Rinehart and Company, 1942); Andre Fontaine, "Are We Staking Our Future on a Crop of Sissies?," *Better Homes and Gardens* (December 1950); Bill Davidson, "Why Half Our Combat Soldiers Fail to Shoot," *Collier's* (November 8, 1952). See also John Costello, *Virtue Under Fire: How World War II Changed Our Social and Sexual Attitudes* (Boston: Little, Brown and Company, 1985).

2. "Truck Convoy," *Battle* 6 (Foto Parade: January 1952), began: "It's June in Korea . . . but don't expect pretty flowers! They can't find the sun . . . because the dead are in the way!" Later came this assertion: "Yelling that you want to get into combat doesn't mean you're a brave man . . . it means you're *foolish*! While you're screaming to get up to the front, every G.I. up on the line is praying and fighting for his life . . . cursing the day he was sent into combat!" The last story in the same issue, "Sneak Attack!," identified Korea as "the playground of death." Stories in which all, or virtually all,

American soldiers died were not uncommon. See "Hit the Dirt!," *Men in Action* 2 (Interstate Publishing: May 1952); "Who's Next?" and "The Final Grave," *War Combat* 3 (Sports Action: July 1952); "Do or Die," *Fighting Front Comics* 1 (Harvey Publications: August 1952); and "The Four Seasons," *Battle Cry* 7 (Stanmor Publications: May—June 1953). These are entirely representative of an abundant body of material.

3. There were other environmental aspects, too, as in "Mud!," *Two-Fisted Tales* 25 (Fables Publishing Company: January—February 1952), and "Muck!," *War Comics* 10 (U.S.A. Comic Magazine Corporation: June 1952).

4. Instructive were "Private Smith" and "The Slaughter on Suicide Hill," *Battlefield* 1 (Animirth Comics: April 1952). In the first, a soldier with an identity crisis said of his name, "It's nuthin' . . . and I'm nuthin'," and, thus preoccupied, was shot to death by enemy troops. In the second, a soldier saw his sergeant's corpse and "felt as if someone had reached down thru my helmet and grabbed my guts and tried to yank 'em up thru my brains." Under orders to carry a message to headquarters, he had to cross a battlefield. "I stepped over the dead . . . I stumbled over 'em . . . fell on top of 'em! There were hundreds of them . . . dead and dying . . . guys I came over from the states with. . . . When I got to battalion, I was covered with blood . . . the smell . . . the sight of all those dead hammered at my brain!" Battle fatigue was the diagnosis, and a hypodermic was the prescription. On the same subject, see "Bug Out!," *Two-Fisted Tales* 24 (Fables Publishing Company: November-December 1951), and "Breakdown," *Man Comics* 24 (Newsstand Publications: March 1953).

5. On officers, see "Chain of Command," *Battlefield* 1; "Torture!," *Bill Battle, The One Man Army* 4 (Fawcett Publications: April 1953); "A Platoon!," *Frontline Combat* 6 (Tiny Tot Comics: May—June 1952). On Red weapons, superior, invincible, secret, or otherwise, see "Operation Massacre," *G.I. Combat* 2 (Comics Magazines: December 1952); *Captain Steve Savage Battles the Red Mystery Jet* 8 (Avon Periodicals: January 1953); "Thunderjet!," *Frontline Combat* 8 (Tiny Tot Comics: September—October 1952); "Silent Death!," *U.S. Paratroopers Surprise Attack* 6 (Avon Periodicals: December 1952). For confusion about the reasons for American involvement, see "Bullets, Babies and Bombs!," *Warfront* 1 (Harvey Features Syndicate: September 1951); and "Foothold!," *Man Comics* 24.

6. "Prisoner of War!," *Frontline Combat* 3 (Tiny Tot Comics: November—December 1951); "Death March," *War Action* 3 (Canon Publishers Sales Corporation: June 1952); "Prison Camp Slaughter," *G.I. Combat* 2.

7. For arrogant Red officers destroyed by Americans, see "The Big Guns!," *Men's Adventures* 16 (Comic Combine Corporation: October 1952), and "The Anger of Colonel Wu-San," *Battle* 4 (Foto Parade: November 1952). For Red troops killing their own officers, see "Glory!," *War Adventures* 6 (Hercules Publishing Corporation: July 1952); "War Lord," *Young Men on the Battlefield* 18 (Interstate Publishing Corporation: December 1952); "The Last Command of Colonel Fong," *Battle* 17 (Foto Parade: Febru-

ary 1953). For Red officers as absurd figures, see "The Command of General Mu," *War Action* 3, and "No Surrender," *G-I in Battle* 9 (Four Star Publications: July 1953). For Red officers lying to their men, see "Red Attack!," *Battle* 12 (Foto Parade: September 1952); "Red Thirteen," *Jumbo Comics* 164 (Real Adventures Publishing Company: October 1952); "Pep Talk!," *Battlefield* 11 (Animirth Comics: May 1953).

8. As in "Bombs Away!," *Fighting Fronts!* 4 (Harvey Publications: November 1952); "True Hero," *War Fury* 1 (Allen Hardy Associates: September 1952).

9. "The Death Trap of General Wu," *Battle* 5 (Foto Parade: November 1951), was among the stories asserting that the Reds were tougher than Americans had supposed.

10. As demonstrated in "Atrocity Story," *War Adventures on the Battlefield* 2 (Animirth Comics: June 1952).

11. For American soldiers as "killing machines," see "The Fighting Machines!," *War Comics* 7 (Comic Magazine Corporation: December 1951); "Blood!," *Battle* 6; and "War Machines," *Frontline Combat* 5 (Tiny Tot Comics: March–April 1952).

12. As in "Bellyrobber!," *Frontline Combat* 6. But such items as "Battle Orphan," *Real Life Comics* 59 (Visual Editions: September 1952), suggested that the humanitarian gesture was not always misplaced.

13. For this favorite theme, see "Enemy Assault!" *Frontline Combat* 1 (Tiny Tot Comics: July–August 1951); "The Enemy Strikes," *Men's Adventures* 12 (Comic Combine Corporation: February 1952); "The Comrade," *Man Comics* 16 (Newsstand Publications: July 1952). The epithet "gook" was not uncommon inside the war books, but rarely did it appear on the cover, as in *G-I in Battle* 9.

14. "Sizzling Pin-Ups!," *G.I. Joe* 14 (Ziff-Davis: August 1952). In "The Lorelei Squadron," *Jet Aces* 3 (Real Adventures Publishing Company: 1952), Mig pilots impersonated women, believing that American males would be too chivalrous to shoot them down. The ploy worked once, but the American fliers eventually won "a psychological victory" in consequence of "seeing through those little tricky deals" for which the Reds were so notorious.

15. Many Americans committed suicide for the cause generally or to save endangered comrades. The suggestion of the cover of *War Comics* 7 was confirmed in "Explosion!," *Men in Action* 2. "Eager Beaver," *Men in Action* 8 (Interstate Publishing Corporation: November 1952), concerned a soldier who called in artillery fire on his position in order to kill Reds. It asked these questions: "What makes a guy a hero? Is it guts? . . . Courage? . . . Luck? . . . Or does a guy have to be plain nuts?"

16. Asiatics in American uniforms were always suspect. In addition to "True Hero," *War Fury* 1, see "Chinese All-American," *Warfront* 12 (Fighting Forces Publications: November 1952), and "Firing Squad," *Men's Adventures* 12.

17. See "Conchie!," *Men in Action* 2, for some attempt to deal with the question.

18. "Light Brigade!," *Frontline Combat* 4 (Tiny Tot Comics: January–February 1952).

19. "Caesar!," *Frontline Combat* 8; "Pigs of the Roman Empire," *Two-Fisted Tales* 21 (Fables Publishing Company: May–June 1951).

20. In this case, the bright covers were those of *Frontline Combat* 10 (Tiny Tot Comics: January–February 1953).

21. "Custer's Last Stand," *Two-Fisted Tales* 27 (Fables Publishing Company: May–June 1952). For contrast, see "Code of the Cavalry!" *War Combat* 4 (Sports Action: September 1952).

22. "Washington!," *Two-Fisted Tales* 29 (Fables Publishing Company: September–October 1952).

23. Harvey Kurtzman, editor of *Two-Fisted Tales* and *Frontline Combat*, demanded the research. "An Interview with the Man Who Brought Truth to the Comics: Harvey Kurtzman," *The Comics Journal* 67 (October 1981).

24. See "Combat Correspondence" pages in *Two-Fisted Tales* 25 (Fables Publishing Co.: January–February 1952) and *Two-Fisted Tales* 27.

25. Wrote Harvey Kurtzman in response to a reader, "Combat Correspondence," *Two-Fisted Tales* 24, "We agree . . . that war is needless. We have no solution. We can only hope that by showing how ugly war is, YOUR generation will work hard to find the solution!"

26. Among countless others, see "Hermit Girl," *Joe Yank* 9 (Visual Editions: December 1952), of interest because it managed to combine politics, sex, an arrogant Red officer, and graphic violence. The rivals here were a private and a sergeant, competing for the affections of a shapely South Korean girl promised by her pro-Communist father to the evil Colonel Blood. The private killed the Red colonel by simultaneously strangling him and smashing his head repeatedly against the floor, before mixing it up with the sergeant again.

27. "Combat Correspondence," *Two-Fisted Tales* 29.

28. See "Lover O'Leary and His Liberty Belles," *Tell It To the Marines* 2 (Toby Press: May 1952); "Gil's Gals," *Fighting Leathernecks* 3 (Toby Press: June 1952); and "Pin-Up Pete," *Monty Hall of the U.S. Marines* 11 (Toby Press: April 1953). *Pin-Up Pete* 1 (Toby Press: 1952) was a blatant vehicle for sexual fantasy. See also the Canteen Kate feature in *Fightin' Marines* 6 (St. John Publishing Company: June 1952). Kate appeared in three issues of her own comic book during 1952. *Buddies in the U.S. Army* 1 (Avon Periodicals: 1952) was the first of two issues concerning "fightin' guys and fabulous gals!" For examples of extravagantly proportioned oriental women of various political persuasions, see *Combat Kelly* 13 (Sphere Publications: May 1953).

29. See the "new, pick-a-boyfriend G.I. listing" in *Wartime Romances* 13 (St. John Publishing Company: January 1953), and the "G.I. Joe's Pen Pals" section in *G.I. Joe* 23 (Ziff-Davis: July 1953), for example.

30. Michael Uslan, ed. and intro., *America at War: The Best of DC War Comics* (New York: Simon and Schuster, 1979), 9. Consider *Battlefront* 19 (Postal Publications: May 1954), containing stories of the Spanish conquest in the sixteenth century, World War I, and World War II. There was but one

Korean War story in this formerly all-Korean comic book—and it was atypical because it was so positive with regard to American valor, leadership, and intellect.

31. "Torture!," *Battle* 12, had expressed the rare hope that tactical atomic weapons would be made available to American troops. For the most part, however, comic books attempted to accustom readers to the idea of limited warfare conducted along traditional lines, as in, for example, "The Infantry's War," *War Comics* 2 (U.S.A. Comic Magazine Corporation: February 1951). The theme was repeated in an unbelievably brutal story, "Tooth and Nail," *War Comics* 13 (U.S.A. Comic Magazine Corporation: November 1952), concerning a "beast-like encounter" between an American corporal and "a big Red officer," even in "this age of automatic weapons . . . long range artillery . . . tanks . . . guided missiles . . . and atomic bombs . . . all this push-button type war." Michael Vlahos has remarked that nuclear weapons "negated the only kind of war that could be considered positive in our national ethos: one that is capable of unifying our national identity. Limited war is almost always unacceptable." And the comic books of the Korean War era underscore the truth of the assertion. See Vlahos, "The End of America's Postwar Ethos," *Foreign Affairs* (Summer 1988), 1095. On occasion, there were comic-book preachments about the expendability of American troops, all for the sake of preserving secret technology, as in "Forced Landing!," *Fighting War Stories* 1 (Mens Publications: August 1952), which might have foreshadowed a new American ethos. Such items as "Capt. Marvel Jr. Battles Vampira, Queen of Terror," *Captain Marvel, Jr.* 20 : 116 (Fawcett Publications: December 1952), indicated the absurdity of having costumed superheroes participate in the Korean conflict.

Chapter 5

1. William W. Savage, Jr., *The Cowboy Hero: His Image in American History and Culture* (Norman: University of Oklahoma Press, 1979), 158–59.

2. The figures are obscure, at best, but evidently there was money to be made from cowboy comic books, probably because of the tie-in factor involving television and other media. *Business Week,* (January 19, 1952): 151, reported that actor William Boyd's share of the take from Hopalong Cassidy comic books issued during 1951 was $55,000.

3. Which is not to say that comic-book writers, artists, and/or editors did not take the occasional startling liberty with what was supposed to be wholesome fare. In "Ghost Town Gun Runners," *Rex Allen* 316 (Dell Publishing Company: February 1951), for example, there were several references to "the Cumload Trail," a venue supposedly in Colorado.

4. See "Roy Rogers Trades Lead," *Roy Rogers Comics* 25 (Dell Publishing Company: January 1950); "Roy Rogers in Mustang Mountain," *Roy Rogers Comics* 27 (Dell Publishing Company: March 1950); "Gene Autry and the Impostors," *Gene Autry Comics* 57 (Dell Publishing Company: November 1951), for example.

5. "Wild Bill Elliott in Medicine Trail," *Wild Bill Elliott Comics* 2 (Dell Pub-

lishing Company: November 1950). For treatment of the drug question in the crime/costumed-hero genre, "The Death Drug!," *Doll Man* 39 (Comic Favorites: April 1952), is an appropriate example; and for the police approach, there is "H Is for Heroin," *Down With Crime* 3 (Fawcett Publications: March 1952).

6. "Rocky Lane and the Extortion Plot," *Six-Gun Heroes* 22 (Fawcett Publications: September 1953).

7. "Mantrap at Broken Butte," *Roy Rogers Comics* 64 (Dell Publishing Company: April 1953).

8. "A Challenge in the Big Bend," *Roy Rogers Comics* 57 (Dell Publishing Company: September 1952).

9. "Poisoned Water," *Roy Rogers Comics* 57.

10. "Medicine Smoke," *Roy Rogers Comics* 64.

11. "Christmas at Corbett's Curve," *Roy Rogers Comics* 61 (Dell Publishing Company: January 1953).

12. "Mountain Mystery," *Roy Rogers Comics* 61.

13. "The Strange Man Hunt," *Roy Rogers Comics* 66 (Dell Publishing Company: June 1953). The times made Rogers jumpy, it would seem. After witnessing men running from a plane crash in "Man's Oldest Weapon," *Roy Rogers Comics* 34 (Dell Publishing Company: October 1950), the cowboy told a comrade, "Get out of range, Frank . . . I've got to risk some shooting to pin those hombres down! They're aliens . . . Maybe spies, too." They turned out to be smugglers.

14. "The Saboteurs," *Buster Crabbe* 12 (Famous Funnies Publications: September 1953); "Bloody Oil," *John Wayne Adventure Comics* 21 (Toby Press: July 1953).

15. See, for example, "Roy Shoots the Works," *Roy Rogers Comics* 36 (Dell Publishing Company: December 1950); "Roy Springs a Trap," *Roy Rogers Comics* 42 (Dell Publishing Company: June 1951); "The Rustler of Goblin Hill," *Roy Rogers Comics* 62 (Dell Publishing Company: February 1953); and "The Mine at Ghost Gulch," *Roy Rogers Comics* 65 (Dell Publishing Company: March 1954).

16. Richard Gid Powers, *G-Man: Hoover's FBI in American Popular Culture* (Carbondale: Southern Illinois University Press, 1983), discusses the policy and its manifestation in every medium except comic books, about which nothing is said.

17. In "The Manhunt for Five," *Roy Rogers Comics* 76 (Dell Publishing Company: April 1954), the hero polished off a gang of moonshiners without any mention of subversives out to corrupt America or to avoid paying federal taxes or anything like that; and the F.B.I. failed to put in an appearance. Times had indeed changed.

Chapter 6

1. The image of the black clown represented by Billy Batson's valet Steamboat and Pokey Jones of the Commando Cubs extended into the post-war period in the person of Ebony, the black waif who was the sometime

aide of the Spirit, but in the immediate postwar years, one could encounter the humorous black in almost any kind of comic book, such as "Zippie," *Thrilling Comics* 69 (Standard Magazines: December 1948); "Floogy," *Crash Comics* 53 (Comic Magazines: March 1948); "Speck, Spot and Sis," *Target Comics* 9 : 4 (Premium Group of Comics: June 1948); and *Mickey Finn* 14 (Publication Enterprises: 1949). See *The Complete Pogo Comics Volume I: Pogo & Albert* (Forestville, Calif.: Eclipse Books, 1989) for Walt Kelly's comic-book stereotypes and Maggie Thompson's justification of them. For Steamboat as a blatant stereotype, see "The Mystery of Lost River," *Captain Marvel Adventures* 36 (Fawcett Publications: June 1944); and for Pokey Jones delivering lines like "Lawdy! We is happened to an accident," en route to an atypical combat role in the war in Europe, see "Commando Cubs," *Thrilling Comics* 36 (Better Publications: July 1943). The Spirit appeared in a weekly comic book distributed by many newspapers as a Sunday supplement from 1940 to 1952 and enjoyed other comic-book manifestations through the mid-1950s. Several postwar Ebony stories were reprinted in magazine format in *The Spirit* 7 (April 1975), by which time such things were understandably controversial. Will Eisner, the creator-artist-writer of the Spirit stories, has taken pains to explain—but, to his credit, not to excuse—the Ebony character as a stereotypical product of the social climate of the 1940s. Indeed, he has not been allowed to forget the situation, owing to the status of the Spirit stories as classic comic art and the frequency with which the work is reprinted. His comments are available in several places, but see Dave Schreiner, "Stage Settings: Struggling with Destiny," *The Spirit* 26 (Kitchen Sink Press: December 1986), and "Stage Settings: Sam Spade and the Nature Boy," *The Spirit* 32 (Kitchen Sink Press: June 1987), as well as "Catch the Spirit: An Interview with Will Eisner," *Four-Color Magazine* 1 : 2 (January 1987): 28–34, 66.

2. There were a few short-lived comic books issued by mainstream publishers for black audiences in the postwar period, as *Negro Romance* from Fawcett Publications (three issues, June to October 1950), but all were discontinued, probably because of poor sales.

3. "Bunker!," *Two-Fisted Tales* 30 (Fables Publishing Company: November–December 1952), marked a rare appearance of black troops in a war comic, although they could be found occasionally in documentary-style comic books in connection with service in Korea. See, for example, "Sgt. Charlton and Hill 543," *New Heroic Comics* 74 (Famous Funnies Publications: August 1952). In the absence of editorial comment upon blackness, the documentary comic books allowed the art to indicate ethnicity, leading to a certain amount of ambiguity.

4. The racist tendencies of some writers and editors could hardly have been more blatantly exhibited. For example, in "Savage Titan," *Terrors of the Jungle* 5 (Star Publications: June 1953), a white heroine, warning hunters away from forbidden land, identified herself by announcing, "I am Nigah, queen of the jungle!" There was at least one black jungle hero, whose name was Voodah (as in Voodoo or, perhaps, Doo-dah), and who, in "Voodah,"

Crown Comics 5 (Golfing, Inc.: 1945), managed to kill a thawed *Tyrannosaurus rex* with only a dagger; but he was neither king nor lord nor any other titled personage.

5. The volume of evidence is overwhelming, but see "The Land of the Black Python," *Thrilling Comics* 66 (Standard Magazines: June 1948), wherein a white Princess Pantha taught black Africans to overcome racial prejudice in a near-classic example of "blame-the-victim" mentality; "The Man Who Wouldn't Die," *Rulah* 23 (Fox Feature Syndicate: February 1949), wherein a white jungle "goddess" (Rulah was a ruler, don't you see) had to deal with a dying white man who had decided to amuse himself by encouraging suicide among natives who ignorantly believed that he was relaying messages from their gods; and "The Headhunters of Bullah," *White Princess of the Jungle* 4 (Avon Periodicals: August 1952), wherein "fierce fighters" who were "such simple children" begged the forgiveness of white Princess Taanda for having been hoodwinked by an unscrupulous white man who paraded as their god and had them doing vile things. Blacks routinely begged for white forgiveness, as in "Fire Rain," *Zoot* 16 (Fox Feature Syndicate: July 1948), which featured ex-Nazis trying to take over Rulah's jungle by exploiting superstitious natives; and "The Golden Ghost Gorilla," *Terrors of the Jungle* 19 (Star Publications: October 1952), in which blacks prostrated themselves before a white "Congo king" who had saved them from the sort of disaster that follows the worship of false idols. Sheena, the archetypal female counterpart of Tarzan, regularly saved her native wards from the designs of evil whites—see the untitled Sheena story in *Jumbo Comics* 129 (Real Adventures Publishing Company: November 1949), for example—as well as the plots of devious blacks, as in the third untitled story in *Sheena* 13 (Real Adventures Publishing Company: Fall 1951). Even children, if they were white, could manage to set things right for blacks who had fallen prey to their own foolishness. See the first and second untitled stories in *Wambi, Jungle Boy* 10 (Glen-Kel Publishing Company: 1950). Movie stars had their chance to be pale and superior as well, as in "Vengeance of the Panther King," *Dorothy Lamour* 2 (Hero Books, Inc.: June 1950), which concluded with blacks begging forgiveness from Hollywood's "jungle princess." That white lords and ladies of the jungle unabashedly interfered with tribal customs and tribal politics whenever they pleased was demonstrated in "The Wickedness of Gogulu," *Edgar Rice Burrough's Tarzan* 28 (Dell Publishing Company: January 1952); the untitled Kaanga story in *Jungle Comics* 153 (Glen-Kel Publishing Company: September 1952); and "The Ghost Walked at Midnight," *Lorna, the Jungle Girl* 8 (Official Magazine Corporation: July, 1954).

6. Among other things, blacks never seemed to learn to avoid fooling around with white women, especially if they were the property of some white jungle king. This was less a comment upon their persistence than an assertion of their stupidity. Cover art usually spilled the beans. Among many examples, see *Jungle Comics* 77 (Glen-Kel Publishing Company: May 1946), and *Jungle Comics* 94 (Glen-Kel Publishing Company: October 1947), which

indicated that either black males or black females could do the fooling around.

7. Communists showed up in "Jungle Guns," *Wild Boy* 10 (Ziff-Davis Publishing Company: 1950), despite its number the first in the series; "Seeds of Slaughter," *Police Comics* 114 (Comic Magazines: April 1952); and "The Army of Terror," *White Princess of the Jungle* 3 (Avon Periodicals: May 1952), whereas ex-Nazis menaced the natives in "Fire Rain," *Zoot* 16; "The Tyrant of the Jungle," *Wild Boy* 4 (Ziff-Davis Publishing Company: October–November 1951); and "Exile Dangerous," *Terrors of the Jungle* 21 (Star Publications: February 1953). A crackpot atomic scientist sought to rule pygmies and make billions from a secret nuclear process in "Lord of the Little People," *Thun'da* 5 (Magazine Enterprises: 1953). Blacks were always willing to listen to any sort of political mumbo jumbo, and it was not surprising that Tarzan himself should have to deal with Mau-Mau terrorism in "The Mark of Evil," *Edgar Rice Burroughs' Tarzan* 50 (Dell Publishing Company: November 1953), as did the blond bombshell, Cave Girl, in "The Mau Mau Killers," *Cave Girl* 13 (Magazine Enterprises: July–September 1954); and, given the colonialist perspective inherent in the material, anticolonialism *had* to be mumbo jumbo, devoid of any meaningful political or philosophical nuance. In contrast to jungle comics, the western books often preached that the most effective "natives" were in reality white men, as in *Straight Arrow* (fifty-five issues, Magazine Enterprises, 1950–1956), translated from the radio character developed to flog Nabisco Shredded Wheat in 1949, and such offerings as *Apache Kid* (nineteen issues, Medalion Publishing Corporation and Canam Publishing Sales Corporation, 1950–1956).

8. Or at least not until white folks ran afoul of it, which was usually the case in horror comics when cynical whites scoffed at some tribal superstition and wound up having the devil to pay, so to speak. "Two Must Die," *Ghost Comics* 6 (Superior Publishers: 1953), expressed such a theme—and coincidentally characterized contemporary Mexicans as "natives."

9. Sheena, for all her moxie in dealing with blacks, was forever being dealt sharp blows to the back of the head. If she did not revive by falling in a river, she had to be saved by her pet monkey or her white "mate." Instructive are the three untitled stories in *Sheena, Queen of the Jungle* 9 (Real Adventures Publishing Company: 1950), wherein the heroine, twice clubbed to the ground and once pistol-whipped, demonstrated just how thick one human skull could be. Señorita Rio ("Queen of the Spies"), who began appearing in *Fight Comics* in 1942, and Firehair (the "Frontier Queen"), who premiered in *Ranger Comics* in 1945, were Sheena's sisters, having come from the Iger Studios for publication under the Fiction House umbrella. Señorita Rio was smarter than Sheena, and Firehair was tougher; but Sheena was typical. There were other, but rare and relatively short-lived exceptions to the weak-sister image among heroines devoid of super powers, as in "Phantom Pirates of the Bay," *National Comics* 60 (Comic Magazines: June 1947), concerning policewoman Sally O'Neil, who could beat several grown men at a time into submission without help.

10. See Will Eisner, "Women as They Are Portrayed in Comics," *Comics Collector* 7 (Spring 1985): 32, and Maurice Horn, *Women in the Comics* (New York: Chelsea House, 1980) chs. 5 and 6. See also Martha Saxton, *Jayne Mansfield and the American Fifties* (Boston: Houghton Mifflin Company, 1975), required reading in this context. Trina Robbins and Catherine Yronwode, *Women and the Comics* (N.p.: Eclipse Books, 1985), ch. 4, treat the employment of women in the comic-book industry but make no attempt to deal with the sexist content of the material or to explain women's contributions to their own stereotyping. There was probably not anything approaching a "women's movement" in the 1940s and 1950s with sufficient influence to counter such imagery, but see Leila J. Rupp and Verta Taylor, *Survival in the Doldrums: The American Women's Rights Movement, 1945 to the 1960s* (New York: Oxford University Press, 1987). For a rare treatment of male sexism in comics intended for boys, see the Dick Cole story in *4 Most* 7 : 4 (Premium Group of Comics: July–August 1948).

11. See the discussion in Naomi Scott, *Heart Throbs: The Best of DC Romance Comics* (New York: Simon and Schuster, 1979), 9–12. Richard Howell, ed., *Real Love: The Best of the Simon and Kirby Romance Comics: 1940s–1950s* (Forestville, Calif.: Eclipse Books, 1988), offers examples of the genre either drawn and written by, or prepared under the supervision of, Jack Kirby and Joe Simon, the prewar creators of Captain America and other hero-related titles. Their romance stories centered on adult "affairs" rather than the romantic concerns of teenagers, and contained a fair amount of social commentary. Women tended to fare better in newspaper comic strips, where heroes (e.g., Dick Tracy, Joe Palooka) were sometimes married men, especially in the late 1940s. Strips are largely the domain of Robbins and Yronwode, *Women and the Comics.*

12. See Maggie Thompson, "Little Ms. Moppet," *Comics Collector* 2 (Winter 1984): 67–72, and "Little Ms. Moppet, Part II," *Comics Collector* 3 (Spring 1984): 67–71, a telling appreciation.

13. The classic format for her stories involved boy-girl versions of the war between the sexes and generally resulted in boys losing their pants. Compare "The Picnic Pirates," *Marge's Little Lulu* 23 (Dell Publishing Company: May 1950), and "Five Little Babies," *Marge's Little Lulu* 38 (Dell Publishing Company: August 1951). Marge was Marjorie Henderson Buell, who had developed Little Lulu for *Saturday Evening Post* in a series of weekly panels that began in 1935. The comic-book version was largely the work of a man, John Stanley.

14. Although, once again, writers and editors sometimes took matters into their own hands by exhibiting a certain perversity inappropriate to the genre. In the early 1950s, for example, *Popular Teen-Agers* offered the antics of a young lady named Toni Gay and her young male companion, one Butch Dykeman, which may be taken, one supposes, as an indication of stress on somebody's part. Dean Mullaney, ed., *Teen-Aged Dope Slaves and Reform School Girls* (Forestville, Calif.: Eclipse Books, 1989), reprints eight atypical comic-book stories from the period 1947–1954 concerning teenage involve-

ment with crime, drugs, and venereal disease—atypical because the most lurid were either from one-shot comic books or from educational comics issued by such institutions as Columbia University. Ageism is the device that carried *Gabby Hayes Western* through fifty issues for Fawcett Publications between 1948 and 1953. If the old (and often even the middle-aged) were not buffoons, then they were weak and (like children) in need of the services of able-bodied heroes no older than thirty-five.

15. "The Next Job," *Shock Suspenstories* 1 (Tiny Tot Comics: February–March 1952); "Well-Traveled," *Shock Suspenstories* 5 (Tiny Tot Comics: October–November 1952); "The Orphan," *Shock Suspenstories* 14 (Tiny Tot Comics: April–May 1954).

16. "The Small Assassin!," *Shock Suspenstories* 7 (Tiny Tot Comics: February–March 1953), based on a Ray Bradbury short story from 1946, the year of publication of Dr. Spock's *The Common Sense Book of Baby and Child Care.*

17. "Just Desserts," *Shock Suspenstories* 3 (Tiny Tot Comics: June–July, 1952).

18. "Sugar 'n Spice 'n . . . ," *Shock Suspenstories* 6 (Tiny Tot Comics: December 1952–January 1953); "Stumped," *Shock Suspenstories* 3.

19. As in "Fantastic Brain Destroyers," *Zip-Jet* 1 (St. John Publishing Company: February 1953), featuring a demented psychiatrist who forced inmates of an asylum to imbibe radioactive calcium, by way of creating a few dozen monsters. Or consider the goofy professionals who fed radioactive salt to a condemned killer to see if people could develop "immunity to radioactive poisoning" in "Captain Marvel and the Radioactive Man," *The Marvel Family* 22 (Fawcett Publications: April 1948).

20. See "Meet the Split Benny Dickson! Public Enemy #1," *True Crime Comics* 3 (Magazine Village: July–August 1948), for all the customary gambits.

21. "Lead-Slinging Bride," *Outlaws* 1 (D. S. Publishing Company: February–March 1948), taught that several wrongs could make a right, and that a man who turned to crime for the fun of it could escape prosecution with a little help from his girl friend. *Outlaws* was a western title. Within the western genre there were many offerings concerning the deeds of "good" badmen, for example, *Jesse James*, published by Avon Periodicals (twenty-nine issues and one annual, 1950–1956), and *Billy the Kid Adventure Magazine*, published by Toby Press (thirty issues, 1950–1955).

22. Kip Burland, a uniformed policeman, became a costumed hero called Black Hood, frequently for no good reason, as indicated in "The Black Hood and the Case of the Blood Red Rubies," *Black Hood Comics* 15 (M. L. J. Magazines: Summer 1945).

Chapter 7

1. See the discussion in Henry E. Schultz, "Censorship or Self Regulation?," *The Journal of Educational Sociology* 23 : 4 (December 1949): 215–24. Some comic-book publishers sought to stem the tide of parental criticism

by retaining "editorial boards" of experts in the fields of psychology and psychiatry, education, English literature, child guidance, and reading. As a rule, the larger the publishing company, the longer the roster of experts. National Comics Publications (or D.C.) boasted a five-member board in 1949. At the same time, the nascent Marvel Comic Group had only one "editorial consultant," albeit a psychiatrist. For statements of the issues from publishers' perspectives, see the "Hi Friends" letter in *Sub Mariner Comics* 30 (Manvis Publications: February 1949), and "A letter to our readers and their PARENTS!," *All Western Winners* 4 (Current Detective Stories: April 1949). While most publishers tried to emphasize the illogic of equating comic-book reading with delinquency, at least one, Lev Gleason, turned the argument around and suggested that reading *his* books caused a decrease in delinquent behavior. See the centerfold in *Crime Does Not Pay* 65 (Lev Gleason Publications: July 1948). Some Gleason books were near-perfect anticrime tracts, and among the best was *Daredevil* 50 (Lev Gleason Publications: September 1948), designed to convey to adolescents the importance of making the right choices in life.

2. Fredric Wertham, *Seduction of the Innocent* (New York: Holt, Rinehart and Winston, 1954).

3. See James Gilbert, *A Cycle of Outrage: America's Reaction to the Juvenile Delinquent in the 1950s* (New York: Oxford University Press, 1986), the sixth chapter of which concerns Wertham and comic books.

4. Such a perspective is expressed in Carter Scholz, "Seduction of the Ignorant," *The Comics Journal* 80 (March 1983), 48–53. Gilbert, *A Cycle of Outrage*, portrays a serious Wertham, sincere in his criticisms.

5. Wertham, *Seduction*, 265.

6. Ibid., 189–90.

7. Ibid., 192–93.

8. "The Guilty," *Shock Suspenstories* 3; "In Gratitude . . . ," *Shock Suspenstories* 11 (Tiny Tot Comics: October–November 1953); "Hate," *Shock Suspenstories* 5 (Tiny Tot Comics: October–November 1952). See also "Blood Brothers," *Shock Suspenstories* 13 (Tiny Tot Comics: February–March 1954).

9. The discussion that follows is based on Frank Jacobs, *The Mad World of William M. Gaines* (Secaucus, N.J.: Lyle Stuart, 1972), and "An Interview with William M. Gaines," *The Comics Journal* 81 (May 1983), 53–84.

10. "The Patriots," *Shock Suspenstories* 2 (Tiny Tot Comics: April–May 1952); "Under Cover," *Shock Suspenstories* 6 (Tiny Tot Comics: December 1952–January 1953); "The Whipping," *Shock Suspenstories* 14 (Tiny Tot Comics: April–May 1954).

11. See "Are You a Red Dupe?," *Shock Suspenstories* 16 (Tiny Tot Comics: August–September 1954).

12. The code is appended to Maurice Horn, ed., *The World Encyclopedia of Comics* (New York: Chelsea House, 1976).

13. "A Special Editorial," *Shock Suspenstories* 18 (Tiny Tot Comics: December 1954–January 1955).

14. I accept the figures in Russell Nye, *The Unembarrassed Muse: The*

Popular Arts in America (New York: The Dial Press, 1970), 239–40, as a mere matter of convenience. There appear to be few data, and consensus is not possible. Gilbert, *A Cycle of Outrage*, ch. 6, accepts the notion of a postwar industry output of sixty million copies per month, a figure first advanced by Wertham (*Seduction*, 11) and subsequently repeated by the fourth estate as an accurate estimate.

15. See Gilbert, *A Cycle of Outrage*, ch. 9.

16. Stan Lee, *Origins of Marvel Comics* (New York: Simon and Schuster 1974) and *Son of Origins of Marvel Comics* (New York: Simon and Schuster, 1975), reveal something of the blatant hucksterism typical of the period.

17. Wertham, *Seduction*, 28.

18. Reaction abroad was something else again, especially after the export of Uncle Scrooge (a 1952 comic-book creation) in translations of Disney comics. See Ariel Dorfman and Armand Mattelart, *How to Read Donald Duck: Imperialist Ideology in the Disney Comic* (London: International General, 1975), and Ariel Dorfman, *The Empire's Old Clothes: What the Lone Ranger, Babar, and Other Innocent Heroes Do to Our Minds* (New York: Pantheon Books, 1983), ch. 2.

19. Will Jacobs and Gerard Jones, in *The Comic Book Heroes: From the Silver Age to the Present* (New York: Crown Publishers, 1985), 151–61, offer 1970 as the closing date for the "silver age" and assert that comic books flirted with "relevance" from 1970 to 1972, but that it was only "a passing trend." In regard to the social, political, and economic implications of the medium, Jacobs and Jones have ably demonstrated just how little the post-1954 comic books have thus far brought to mind.

20. The attitude is that technology cannot be controlled, and so its transmissions must be censored. Therefore, if television programming can be made bland, no American will have to be inconvenienced to make the superhuman effort to change channels or turn off the set.

21. Frederic M. Thrasher, "The Comics and Delinquency: Cause or Scapegoat?," *The Journal of Educational Sociology* 23 : 4 (December 1949): 195. Thrasher understood, five years before the appearance of *Seduction of the Innocent*, that Wertham's view was "more forensic than . . . scientific."

Chapter 8

1. Warner Brothers, a studio known for its cartoons featuring Bugs Bunny, Daffy Duck, Porky Pig, Elmer Fudd, and others, exemplified various cases in point. Built upon a cartoon series about Bosko, a stereotypical black youngster who first appeared on the screen in 1930, Warner Brothers' offerings (which were likely to be seen in theatres years after their original release) included *Clean Pastures* (1937), a parody of the 1936 film, *The Green Pastures*, and *Coal Black and de Sebben Dwarfs* (1942), a parody of Disney's 1938 *Snow White and the Seven Dwarfs*. More insidious, perhaps, were pieces like *All This and Rabbit Stew* (1941), wherein Bugs Bunny's foil was not Fudd or the pig or the duck, but a Stepin-Fetchitesque black youngster. As well, Warner Brothers produced a cartoon series about a young cannibal

named Inki which extended into the late 1940s. Indians were stereotyped in, for example, *Slightly Daffy* (1944), and *A Feather in His Hare* (1948); Mexicans in *Mexican Joyride* (1947); and women in nearly everything, but see *Book Revue* (1946). Other cartoon studios might be tarred with the same brush. The Warner Brothers cartoons are particularly obvious, however, owing to videotape re-releases of so much of the material in the past five years.

2. Working as a journalist twenty-five years ago, I heard many stories from career newspapermen about editors and publishers having to censor installments of Al Capp's "Li'l Abner" comic strip on account of what they called "pornography." They had been keeping an eye on Capp since the 1940s, when his hillbilly females began to exhibit more fully developed secondary sex characteristics.

3. Nor can it yet, if the tenor of appreciations like Leonard Maltin, *Of Mice and Magic: A History of American Animated Cartoons* (New York: McGraw-Hill Book Company, 1980), is to be considered typical.

4. See Douglass Cater and Stephen Strickland, *TV Violence and the Child: The Evolution and Fate of the Surgeon General's Report* (New York: Russell Sage Foundation, 1975), for a survey of the period 1954–1974. A useful review of the empirical literature is H. J. Eysenck and D. K. B. Nias, *Sex, Violence and the Media* (New York: Harper Colophon, 1979). Donald Bowie, *Station Identification: Confessions of a Video Kid* (New York: M. Evans and Company, 1980), is a representative memoir.

Bibliographical Note

Anyone contemplating the use of comic books to illuminate aspects of the American experience since the 1930s faces difficulty. M. Thomas Inge, in "Comic Art," an essay in M. Thomas Inge, ed., *Handbook of American Popular Culture*, vol. 1 (Westport, Conn.: Greenwood Press, 1978), 77–102, has noted the paucity of research collections available to investigators. This suggests the low esteem in which most libraries have held comic books, despite the extremes to which they might be willing to go in order to preserve other significant but somehow more dignified ephemeral literature. Libraries that do possess materials cannot be said to have acquired their holdings in any systematic manner. The exception is the Michigan State University Library, which houses the Russel B. Nye Popular Culture Collection containing approximately 45,000 comic books. Even the collection of comic books in the ordinarily reliable Library of Congress is, as Inge remarks, in deplorable condition—in consequence of theft more than anything else, one supposes. A revised version of Inge's essay, together with an updated bibliography, can be found in M. Thomas Inge, ed., *Handbook of American Popular Literature* (Westport, Conn.: Greenwood Press, 1988), 75–99, under the title "Comic Books."

The best and most complete collections of comic books

are in private hands and generally inaccessible to researchers. Therefore, anyone interested in the study of comic books had best be prepared to become a collector; and anyone interested in becoming a collector had best be prepared for inordinate expenditures of time and money. The researcher's advantage in this regard is that a comic book's condition largely determines the price a dealer is paid for it, and if the buyer's concerns lie with content rather than appearance, he or she should be able to find affordable material. Because even the most tattered copy of a pre-1955 comic book is likely to sell in the $3–$5 range, the expense involved in developing a representative collection of, say, a thousand comic books is considerable. Mike Benton's *Comic Book Collecting for Fun and Profit* (New York: Crown Publishers, 1985) can assist the uninitiated.

Any researcher working with comic books must acknowledge the contribution of Robert M. Overstreet, who has published a price guide for collectors annually since 1970. The edition I have used is the seventeenth: Robert M. Overstreet, *The Official Overstreet Comic Book Price Guide, 1987–1988* (New York: The House of Collectibles, 1987). Ostensibly concerned with establishing values of books for dealers and collectors, the *Guide*, as it is commonly known, is actually the most complete index available for comic books (or anything resembling a comic book) published in the United States since 1900. That it is incomplete and contains intentional errors (to thwart plagiarists hoping to offer their own price guides for the collectors' market) has been suggested by Laurence Watt-Evans, "Lost in the Mists: Comics That Don't Exist," *Comics Collector* 10 (Winter 1986): 70–71. To this sort of thing there may be no convenient resolution. Watt-Evans asserted, for example, that *Fighting Undersea Commandos* 1 (Avon Periodicals: 1952) does not exist; and yet the seventeenth edition of the *Guide* still indicates that it does. Watt-Evans' contention that the *Guide* is "surely better than 95% accurate" may be some consolation.

Perhaps because collectors (fans, they are sometimes called) dominate what passes for the "study" of comic books, there is a proprietary air about every enterprise. Thus it is *The Official Overstreet Comic Book Price Guide*—as opposed to, may we ask, an unofficial one? to another "official" one by somebody else? Many of the histories of the medium qualify as "popular"—the antithesis, we understand, of "academic"— and they contain no known documentary apparatus to sustain them. These are generally identified by proprietary titles, as in the cases of James Steranko, *The Steranko History of Comics*, 2 vols. (Wyomissing, Pa.: Supergraphics, 1970–1972); Ron Goulart, *Ron Goulart's Great History of Comic Books* (Chicago: Contemporary Books, 1986); and Hubert H. Crawford, *Crawford's Encyclopedia of Comic Books* (Middle Village, N.Y.: Jonathan David Publishers, 1978). The various essays in Dick Lupoff and Don Thompson, eds., *All in Color for a Dime* (New York: Ace Books, 1970), are generally fan appreciations of noted costumed heroes, but they at least emphasize context. Taken with Don Thompson and Dick Lupoff, eds., *The Comic-Book Book* (New Rochelle, N.Y.: Arlington House, 1973), a better use of the same approach, they represent, with the titles above, considerable improvement on Coulton Waugh, *The Comics* (New York: The Macmillan Company, 1947), and Stephen Becker, *Comic Art in America: A Social History of the Funnies, the Political Cartoons, Magazine Humor, Sporting Cartoons, and Animated Cartoons* (New York: Simon and Schuster, 1959), regardless of how much they may leave to be desired. M. Thomas Inge is one who believes that objective scholarship is possible in general reference works, but in the meantime, Maurice Horn, ed., *The World Encyclopedia of Comics* (New York: Chelsea House, 1976) is the best that researchers are likely to find.

Periodical literature is almost exclusively oriented to the minimal requirements of collectors and fans, and most are obsessed with modern superheroes. New titles come and go with greater regularity than is likely to be exhibited by the publication schedules of the more stable periodicals, and researchers are advised to check the annual listing in the *Guide* to learn what is currently available. *The Comics Journal* is the major periodical, and it may or may not appear monthly. Its principal concern is the criticism of current comic books, but occasionally it publishes interviews with artists, editors, or publishers associated with the pre-1954 period. The *Journal's* companion publication is *Nemo: The Classic Comics Library*, another monthly magazine appearing erratically. *Nemo's* concerns are supposed to be historical, and it reprints a great many old newspaper strips; but documentation is usually absent, to the extent that one may not even discern the provenance of some of the material.

There are many collections of comic-book reprints, but the best, because of the commentaries provided by their editors, are Jules Feiffer, comp., intro., and anno., *The Great Comic Book Heroes* (New York: The Dial Press, 1965), and Michael Barrier and Martin Williams, eds., *A Smithsonian Book of Comic-Book Comics* (New York: Smithsonian Institution Press and Harry N. Abrams, 1981), although the provenance of the reprinted material is handled casually at best.

Fredric Wertham's *Seduction of the Innocent* (New York: Holt, Rinehart and Winston, 1954) deserves particular notice for several reasons. It was the first volume to be devoted exclusively to a discussion of American comic books; and it was the critique of the medium most responsible for forcing changes within the comic-book industry that substantially altered comic-book content. It contains no references, and in consequence of that, there is, among collectors, a regular cottage industry devoted to attempting the identification of the comic books about which Wertham wrote. So, while *Seduction of the Innocent* is useless as history, it is essential to an understanding of the era that produced it. In addition, *Seduction of the Innocent* served, however ironically, as precedent for much of the subjectivity that has passed for comic-book criticism since 1954. Wertham's approach is reflected in such offerings as Arthur Asa Berger, *The Comic-Stripped American: What Dick Tracy, Blondie, Daddy Warbucks, and Charlie Brown Tell Us About Ourselves* (New York: Walker and Company, 1973), and may be said to represent a genre of commentary perhaps best characterized as hoodoo sociology—a jargon-laden admixture of sociology, psychology, and literary criticism. Indeed, scholars of "popular culture" (a worthwhile field of study, but questionably a distinct academic discipline) tend to be persons with doctorates in English, which means that they are grounded in precepts of literary criticism (involving some number of Freudian playthings) and are likely to parse every text according to standards established for the professional consideration of *Moby-Dick*. The resulting subjective analyses of content minimize or ignore the provenance and thus the historical context of whatever happens to be under discussion, probably to obscure the fact that the subject matter constitutes what Jules Feiffer, in order to explain its appeal, aptly termed "junk." Add to this the compulsion of popular culturists of whatever persuasion to find an appropriate methodology, and the utility of the product is further diminished. The outstanding exception to such conventions is Russel Nye, *The Unembarrassed Muse: The Popular Arts in America* (New York: The Dial Press, 1970), splendid history by a professor of English.

Any number of historical studies of the period from the Depression to the mid-1950s have either ignored comic books or failed to recognize their perspective. I have identified in the notes the prominent recent examples touching upon topics of concern here. James Gilbert, *A Cycle of Outrage: America's Reaction to the Juvenile Delinquent in the 1950s* (New York: Oxford University Press, 1986) reflects the mentality in an astonishing manner. Dealing with Wertham and his analyses, Gilbert evidently felt no need actually to look at any comic books of the 1950s. The arguments that popular culture supported consensus and conformity, developed by Douglas Miller and Marion Nowak, *The Fifties: The Way We Really Were* (Garden City, N.Y.: Doubleday and Company, 1977), and Peter Biskind, *Seeing Is Believing: How Hollywood Taught Us To Stop Worrying and Love the Fifties* (New York: Pantheon Books, 1983), are called to question by the themes and messages of many pre-1954 comic books. If omissions may be excused in these and other volumes, it would probably be on the grounds that the material is simply unavailable for perusal in most of the places where people go to do research. Paul A. Carter, *Another Part of the Fifties* (New York: Columbia University Press, 1983), xi, dealt in part with "the attempt by Americans in the fifties to tell each other (and the world) who they were and where they thought they were going" by examining paperback science-fiction novels. There is no mention of comic books or Dr. Wertham. In other words, one does what one can to hasten the day when some grand synthesis of the period's culture may be possible, and when surveys like Melvyn Dubofsky and Athan Theoharis, *Imperial Democracy: The United States since 1945*, 2d ed. (Englewood Cliffs, N.J.: Prentice-Hall, 1988), or John Patrick Diggins, *The Proud Decades: America in War and in Peace, 1941–1960* (New York: W. W. Norton & Company, 1988), will profit therefrom.

The comic books cited in this volume were begged, borrowed, or bought (and usually that) from dealers in Oklahoma, Kansas, Texas, and California over a period of ten years. At the conclusion of the study, I offered my collection of comic books to the library of my choice, only to receive a firm refusal. I now intend to store the books for transmission to my heirs as a hedge against inflation. Perhaps, if my heirs should require no such hedge, they may at some later date ask whether scholarship cares to be served yet.

Index

149

Index